# CONTEMPORARY MEXICAN DESIGN AND ARCHITECTURE

# CONTEMPORARY MEXICAN DESIGN AND ARCHITECTURE

KHRISTAAN VILLELA

ELLEN BRADBURY

LOGAN WAGNER

Gibbs Smith, Publisher
Salt Lake City

First Edition
06 05 04 03 02    5 4 3 2 1

Published by
Gibbs Smith, Publisher
P.O. Box 667
Layton, Utah 84041

Orders: (1-800) 748-5439
www.gibbs-smith.com

Designed and produced by Kate Tsosie, William Field Design
Printed and bound in Hong Kong

Library of Congress Cataloging-in-Publication Data

Villela, Khristaan.
   Contemporary Mexican design and architecture / Khristaan Villela, Ellen
Bradbury, and Logan Wagner.— 1st ed.
        p. cm.
Includes bibliographical references.
   ISBN 1-58685-088-1
1. Architecture, Domestic—Mexico. 2. Architecture, Modern—20th century.
3. Architect-designed houses—Mexico.  I. Bradbury, Ellen. II.
Wagner, Logan. III. Title.
NA7244 .V55 2002
728'.37'097209045—dc21
                                                   2002005187

# CONTENTS

# ACKNOWLEDGEMENTS

This book is the result of a collaborative process between many people. Publisher Gibbs Smith first suggested the topic a couple of years ago. All three authors have been traveling to Mexico for their entire lives—as visitors and later for professional reasons—and two were born in Mexico City. During the past three years, as we traveled to Mexico we bought new books on Mexican architecture and design—including homes, churches, haciendas, tile-work, and even Mexican color—which piled up in our libraries. But we also noticed that with the exception of a few classic treatments of Mexican design, the North American architectural book market was not keeping up with the pace south of the border. There was a growing interest in Mexican architecture outside Mexico. Luis Barragán won the Pritzker Prize in 1980, Ricardo Legorreta earned the gold medal of the American Institute of Architects in 2000, and Villela works at the College of Santa Fe in a complex designed and built in 1999 by Legorreta.

Together we worked on the selection of architects and the book content. Wagner, a Mexican architect, contacted the architects and worked closely with their firms. He obtained most of the images and plans reproduced in this book directly from the files of the architects. We are grateful to all the architects and firms who cooperated with us in this venture: Jorge Alessio Robles, Isaac Broid, José Luis Esquerra, Agustín Hernández, Teodoro González de León, J. B. Johnson, Legorreta + Legorreta, Enrique Norten, Félix Sánchez, Carlos Santos Maldonado, José de Yturbe, and Abraham Zabludovsky. Special thanks go to J. B. Johnson for being our point man in Mexico City. He accompanied Wagner on visits to most of the architectural firms in Mexico City, and was instrumental in securing images and plans from many architects. Johnson also helped obtain many images for the introduction. Thanks also to Bernardo Barquet and the Colegio de Arquitectos in Mexico City, who early on helped us determine the overall pool of significant and relevant Mexican architects.

We have focused only on domestic architecture, and only on projects that have actually been built. Many of the architects presented also design large public buildings, like Legorreta's Camino Real Hotel in Mexico City, or Zabludovsky and González de León's Colegio de México, also in the capital. We simply had to define the scope of the book to a manageable size. Some of the most important examples of modern Mexican architecture can be found in large public commissions like those mentioned above, and we tried to review the highlights in the introduction.

This is not an academic book, but we have consulted many sources written by leading historians. We used these sources to write a brief history of Mexican architecture from Precolumbian times to the present, found in the introduction. Our introduction is longer than usually found in this kind of book, but as we researched this topic we noticed a lack of concise architectural history of Mexico. Most treatments were buried in specialized texts or in Spanish-language sources.

We want to stress that there are many talented architects whom we were not able to include in the present work. We hope to release future volumes showcasing their contributions to contemporary Mexican architecture. The strength and vigor of Mexican architecture is impressive, and we hope this book will bring it to the attention of a wider audience in the United States.

El Castillo, Chichén Itzá, Yucatán, Mexico, c. A.D. 750–1000. Like many ancient Mexican temples, El Castillo was not built to enclose large spaces or offer protection from the elements. Instead it shaped space and tracked the annual progress of the sun. The Maya, like the later Aztecs, worshipped outdoors and used their architecture to create great ceremonial spaces.

# INTRODUCTION

Since the time of Cortés and the conquistadors, travelers to Mexico have been writing about the landscape and its architecture. From the palace of Montezuma to the townhouses of colonial nobility to country estates, Mexico's brilliant sun and clear skies yielded design solutions that emphasized living both inside and out.

Mexican architecture descends from stock that is both European and American, but these traditions have very different foundations. On the one hand, Precolumbian approaches to space and place shaped the Mexican sensibility. During the colonial era, Mexico's new Spanish masters began building directly upon the ruins of the Aztec cities. Although they brought building technology and styles of Gothic Spain with them, the Spanish found that they had to develop some new forms more appropriate to Mexico's climate and native populations. In the realm of religious architecture, the early friars conceived of many building types unique to the New World. These forms continued to develop throughout the colonial period.

After Mexican independence from Spain in 1821, architects and builders adapted new styles, such as French neoclassicism, to native Mexican traditions, climate, and taste.

Twentieth-century Mexican architects followed the same trends as their colleagues in New York, Paris, and London. Modernist movements—including functionalism, purism, and the later International style of Le Corbusier and Mies van der Rohe—influenced industrial and domestic design in Mexico City. Beginning in the 1930s, Juan O'Gorman, Mathias Goeritz, and Luis Barragán most successfully adapted Euro-American modernism to the realities of building and living in Mexico. During the building boom of the 1950s and 1960s, these architects and the following generation applied Mexican modernism in both rapidly expanding Mexico City and the suburbs. By the 1980s, writers on postmodern Mexican design could discern at least three distinct daughters of modernism south of the border: the colorists, the functionalists, and the architects with distinctive personal visions. *Contemporary Mexican Design and Architecture* presents homes within these three groups, most designed and built during the past fifteen years. All three groups of architects proceed from the same basic visual language of functionalism, with its clean lines, industrial materials, and geometric massing. But they combine these features with lessons learned from the architecture of Precolumbian, colonial, and nineteenth-century Mexico.

1

# TRADITIONS:
# ANCIENT MEXICO

*". . . When we saw all of those cities and villages built in the water, and other great towns on dry land, and that straight and level causeway leading to Mexico, we were astounded. These great towns and temples and buildings rising from the water, all made of stone, seemed like an enchanted vision from the tale of Amadis. Indeed, some of our soldiers asked whether it was not all a dream."* (Adapted from Bernal Díaz del Castillo, *History of the Conquest of Mexico,* translated by J. M. Cohen, 1963: 214.)

Teotihuacán, Mexico. Avenue of the Dead looking north. c. 150-700 A.D. The ancient city of Teotihuacán was organized on a grid with the Avenue of the Dead as its north-south axis, ending at the Pyramid of the Moon, visible in the distance. We now believe that the ancient Teotihuacanos modeled their pyramids after mountains. The shape of the Pyramid of the Moon echoes the extinct Cerro Gordo volcano behind.

For Bernal Díaz del Castillo and the other conquistadores with Cortés, the first glimpse of the Aztec capital city of Tenochtitlán in 1519 seemed like a dream inspired by medieval romance novels. The Spanish could hardly comprehend the scale and order of Montezuma's city, filled as it was with public parks, wide causeways, bustling water canals, markets, a zoo and botanical garden, and fearsome temples. The blood-spattered idols in the Aztec temples and the grisly sacrificial rites that took place there repelled the Catholics. But from Cortés to Bernal Díaz, Spanish eyewitnesses admired many aspects of Aztec civilization. They described the Aztec palaces, markets, streets, and urban scene of Tenochtitlán in glowing terms.

Early Western architecture—from Egypt to Greece to Rome and Byzantium—and Renaissance architecture have striven for ever-larger interior spaces. While the Romans created a miraculous interior space at the Pantheon and the Byzantines of Constantinople built Hagia Sofia, architects in Mexico erected the Temples of the Sun and Moon at Teotihuacán, and Maya architects raised the equally astonishing Pyramid of the Feathered Serpent at Chichén Itzá. But unlike the European temples and churches, these ancient Mexican structures enclosed little interior space. They looked up rather than out, as the European structures did. Although Precolumbian Americans built monumental architecture, they conceived of sacred space outside conventional human architecture. Architecture in temples and platforms instead shaped sacred spaces outdoors. Public rituals at Teotihuacán and Chichén Itzá took place in the plazas below the soaring temples and on the exterior terraces of these structures. Precolumbian temples functioned like vast billboards, advertising to the gathered masses the power and deities of ancient Mexican kings.

While their European contemporaries were making buildings, ancient Mexicans were creating spaces. The European antecedents mentioned above are doubtless familiar to readers. However, the Mexican precedents demonstrate very different conceptual approaches. The impulse to define, control, and sanctify space is as old as Homo sapiens, but Precolumbian Americans worshipped deities who inhabited specific locations, and this fact shaped the organization of the spaces in a unique way. The Aztecs, Mayas, and their neighbors created sacred spaces and consecrated locations. The Europeans built cathedrals and palaces. Ancient Mexicans used their architecture—the human-built landscape—to model the sacred natural landscape, including mountains, caves, and springs.

Mexican dwellings before the Conquest varied from simple thatched huts in the countryside to palaces and apartment buildings in urban areas. Just forty miles from downtown Mexico City, the ruins of Teotihuacán have astonished visitors since the sixteenth century. Although the ruins were never lost or overgrown by jungles, the city's true extent only emerged in the 1960s and 1970s when archaeologists mapped constructions extending over eight square miles. The great north-south axis, the Street of the Dead, is more than three miles long and forms the center of a vast urban grid aligned 15.5 degrees east of north. Even structures miles away from the city center hold true to Teotihuacán's immutable grid. Although

some archaeologists explain the city's orientation as an expression of astronomical alignments, others argue that the Street of the Dead and the Pyramid of the Moon at its northern terminus align instead with Cerro Gordo, the extinct volcano that seems to have been the natural model for Teotihuacán's great pyramids.

Quetzalpapalotl Palace, Teotihuacán, Mexico, c. A.D. 650. Teotihuacán was a true urban center with an elite who lived in palaces inside the ceremonial center. The palaces were built on the urban grid using post-and-lintel technology with small interior spaces. Each compound was organized around small plazas bounded by shaded walkways, which allowed ordinary activities to continue during the heat of the day as well as in the rainy season.

Although Teotihuacanos had built the Pyramids of the Sun and Moon by about A.D. 150, the city reached its greatest extent by A.D. 600, when archaeologists estimate more than 125,000 inhabitants crowded the city center. Few cities in the world at this time could claim

3

Arch at Labna, Yucatán, Mexico. c. A.D. 800. The arch at Labna, a corbel vault soaring nearly twenty feet, was one of the largest ever built by the ancient Maya. The Labna Maya placed the arch at the entrance to the city and at the end of a ceremonial road as well.

above all, open arcades and courtyards. These open arcades and loggias provided both air circulation and shade during the warmest hours of the day. Although nighttime temperatures can dip into the forties at the city's mile-high altitude, ancient Teotihuacanos clearly conducted much of their business and daily life outdoors. But their palaces and residential compounds turned inward in an architecture that emphasized privacy in a busy urban setting.

Several hundred years later and far to the south in Mexico's tropical forests, Maya architecture also shows an interest in living and worshipping outdoors. But unlike Teotihuacán's blank-faced apartment complexes, Maya temples often turned outward. The Maya city of Chichén Itzá on the Yucatán Peninsula reached its apogee by about A.D. 1000. Building on more than a thousand years of history and architecture, the Chichén Maya created massive temples and palaces in several square miles of densely urbanized space. Although the Maya never organized their cities according to a strict urban grid as we see at Teotihuacán, no one who visits Chichén Itzá or Calakmul or even Tikal in neighboring Guatemala would say that these were anything less than true cities. The Maya of Chichén Itzá organized their city around two great sinkholes, viewed as entrances to the underworld from the remotest antiquity. Best known of the two, the Sacred Cenote is a vast well more than a hundred feet wide and about eighty feet deep. Although the Chichén Maya drew water from both wells, they also used them as receptacles for sacred offerings, hurling into the murky waters objects of wood, jade, gold, shell, ceramic, and even sacrificial victims.

as many inhabitants. Private life at Teotihuacán revolved around some 2,000 single-story apartment complexes that occupied the blocks of the city grid. Each averaged 150 to 200 feet on a side, and presented a blank face to the street, with few entrances guaranteeing both protection and privacy. Each structure within these apartment buildings, like most buildings at Teotihuacán, had a flat post-and-lintel roof of light masonry or concrete applied over a system of closely placed beams and cross beams. Other structures may have had simpler pitched roofs of thatch.

Complexes like Atetelco or the Palace of the Quetzalpapalotl include a mixture of living spaces, with shrines and living quarters and,

A great city grew around Chichén's two sacred wells. Visitors today gain little sense of the city's thick urbanism, since most structures away from the main temples and plazas still hide beneath almost impenetrable scrub forest. Nonetheless, archaeologists believe that Chichén included dozens of family compounds of varying sizes, from vast to modest. Each compound comprised a mixture of temples, platforms, and domestic structures, including palaces, where the Chichén Maya lived. Unlike

The Palace, Palenque, Mexico, c. A.D. 650. The Palace at the Maya city of Palenque is organized around three main court-yards surrounded by single-story post-and-lintel stone-masonry structures with corbel vaults. As at Teotihuacán, the Palenque palace features covered walkways for shade and inclement weather.

Teotihuacán, residential compounds at Chichén Itzá and other Maya cities rarely presented a blank wall to the surrounding urban spaces. Perhaps due to lower urban densities, Maya residential compounds were more open

to the city. But within, they featured the same approach to life outdoors as at Teotihuacán. Maya palaces sometimes included dozens of rooms and rose to several stories, but the spaces enclosed were generally small and dark.

Like Teotihuacán, the ancient Maya sometimes built flat roofs. But they occasionally built other profiles, including a Precolumbian version of the mansard roof. One major difference between Teotihuacán and Maya architecture was that the Mayas used corbel arches. Cultures all over the world used the corbel vault or arch to span interior space. From Khmer cities like Angkor Wat in Cambodia to the Mycenaean capitals of mainland Greece, corbels were used to span interior space. But unlike vaults built upon the true arch, corbel vaults are not self-supporting. True arches support themselves, requiring a keystone, and the halves of the arch lean on one another. Corbel vaults rely solely on the weight of the masonry above each half for support. Rather than a keystone, corbels have a cap-stone that serves simply to span the distance between the top of each vault half. Corbel vaults generally yield smaller interior spaces than those spanned by true arches. Precolumbian Americans never used the true arch because theirs was not an architecture of large interior space. With the exception of the city of Palenque, Maya builders showed little interest in exploring how to achieve higher ceilings and lighter interior spaces. Furthermore, archaeology has shown that much of the daily business of the Maya residential compound took place outside in the courtyard and in the open platforms and palace arcades. Most Maya cities are located in a humid tropical climate of moderate to heavy rainfall. Open arcades and courtyards allowed life to go on in all kinds of weather.

Murals at Bonampak, Mexico. c. A.D. 790. Ancient Mexicans decorated the walls of their homes and temples with murals depicting both mythology and history. At Bonampak the Maya king Chan-Muwan commissioned a grand mural program extending through three rooms of small structure. Discovered only in 1946, these murals depict the designation of an heir, a battle, presentation of captives, and life at the court. Colored walls play an important role in both ancient and contemporary Mexican design.

Our impression of ancient Mexican architecture today as monochrome gray stone is far from accurate. Precolumbian Mexicans painted their temples and palaces inside and out with bright colors and murals. Even large structures in many Precolumbian cities were painted red, as were the stucco floors and paved plazas between structures. Red was a sacred color, with associations to the dawn, blood, and living forces. The ancient Mexicans also painted murals under the covered arcades and on the inside walls of their buildings. At Teotihuacán the walls of the temples and palaces are covered with frescoes of mythological and ritual scenes, including gods, warriors, animals, and fantastic beings like the feathered serpent. These scenes formed the backdrop for both

domestic and dynastic rituals. The ancient Mayas painted their most famous and best preserved mural program in the jungles of Chiapas at the city of Bonampak. During the reign of Chan-Muwan in the late eighth century, the Bonampak Maya painted three rooms of a small building with hundreds of figures engaged in court life, dance, and warfare. Far from being purely decorative, these murals painted in bright colors and true stucco commemorated key events in Bonampak's history.

## TRADITIONS: COLONIAL AND NINETEENTH-CENTURY MEXICO

Montezuma's Aztec Empire fell to Spanish and Native American armies by the end of summer 1521. Guatemala's Maya kingdoms collapsed in 1528, and those in Yucatán by 1542. Yet the Mayas, Aztecs, and other Precolumbian peoples did not disappear after the Spanish invasion. In Yucatán alone, more than two million people still speak the Maya language. Although we tend to think of the Conquest of Mexico in cataclysmic terms as the complete extinction of the Precolumbian world, in reality the colonial period was characterized by processes of accommodation between European and Native American ways of life, including architecture.

The best-known examples of architectural adaptation can be found in the churches and convents built by the Spanish friars in Mexico in the second half of the sixteenth century. Franciscan, Dominican, and Augustinian brothers were charged with the task of converting the native masses to Christianity. Few professional architects and builders resided in

Atrium and church façade, Izamal, Yucatán, c. 1550. The Franciscan monastery and church at Izamal was built directly on top of Precolumbian Maya mounds leveled to create the largest atrium in the New World. Izamal presents an excellent example of the architecture of conversion, which was developed by the earliest Catholic friars in Mexico. They realized that ancient Mexicans worshipped outdoors in defined spaces and re-created this effect with walls and small corner chapels. Atriums like those in Izamal could accommodate large crowds of newly converted native Mexicans.

Mexico during the first century after the Conquest. Yet with the help of Native American labor gangs, friars and church officials built massive religious establishments like those at Izamal and Mani in Yucatán and Teposcolula, Yanhuitlan, Huejotzingo, and Ixmiquilpan in central Mexico. In an act symbolizing the spiritual conquest of Mexico, the friars often constructed their religious establishments on the ruined platforms of Precolumbian temples. The Franciscan convent of San Antonio Izamal,

completed by about 1555, rests upon a vast Precolumbian platform.

Although the earliest churches in New Spain were constructed of temporary materials with thatched roofs, by the late 1540s these began to be replaced with more permanent structures made of traditional Mexican building materials like limestone covered with stucco and/or whitewashed. In central Mexico, builders used *tezontle,* a volcanic stone similar to *tufa,* which ranged in color from blood red to hues of green.

Building atop pagan temples not only demonstrated the ascendant position of Christianity, but also allowed the friars to appropriate the locations, since in the Precolumbian world sacredness was associated with place. The ancient Mayas and Aztecs were continually renovating their temples, but they built on top of existing structures because they linked location with sanctity. After the Conquest, particular locations in the natural and man-made landscape retained their importance, even after the construction of a Catholic church. The shrine of the Virgin of Guadalupe in Tepeyac is the best example of this phenomenon, since the earliest oratory was built on the same spot as an ancient temple to Tonántzin, an Aztec fertility and earth goddess. Generally, the sixteenth-century friars built their religious establishments in the style of the Isabelline Gothic. The Renaissance largely bypassed Spain and its American holdings, and there are few examples of pure Renaissance-style religious or secular architecture in Mexico. And so the churches, convents, and cloisters have a medieval feel, with their Gothic-style vaults and arcades.

In addition to building on Precolumbian platforms, the friars also developed other strategies that made Mexico's Native Americans more apt to attend catechism and Mass in the months and years after the first mass baptisms just after the Conquest. As described above, Precolumbian peoples conducted their lives largely outdoors. From markets to altars, most public spaces were uncovered and suited to

Open chapel, Teposcolula, Oaxaca, c. 1550. Like atriums, open chapels were devised by the friars to accommodate large crowds of native Mexicans during the early years of conversion to Catholicism. They functioned like acoustic shells, elevating and amplifying the celebrants of the Mass. Open chapels also took advantage of Precolumbian traditions of outdoor worship, and their concave forms may have reminded native Mexicans of the many caves where they formerly worshipped.

large crowds. Spanish friars quickly grasped this fact and devised new church designs to take advantage of the ways Mexican Native Americans worshipped prior to Cortés. They built open chapels and large atriums in front of the earliest churches. Although atriums were known in Catholic church architecture as early as the fourth century with old St. Peter's in Rome, the friars adapted the form in Mexico in a manner unique to the New World. Izamal has the largest atrium, though they can be found throughout Mexico almost wherever sixteenth-century convents survived later renovations and urban expansion.

Sixteenth-century Mexican church atriums often contained a cross at the center and four small chapels, called *posa chapels,* in the corners. At convents like Calpan and Huejotzingo, both in the state of Puebla, the four chapels and the center cross re-create, perhaps unintentionally, a five-part symbol called a quincunx. Resembling the symbol for five on playing dice, the quincunx was an ancient cosmological symbol in Precolumbian America that mapped the cardinal directions as well as the center axis. The newly converted Mexicans would not have missed this connection, as they were used to living in a world where architecture mapped the most sacred cosmologies. And finally, the sixteenth-century church atriums often contained what were called *capillas abiertas* (open chapels), or *capillas de indios* (Native American chapels). Usually located to the left or right of the principal church façade, the open chapels resembled small band shells. At churches like Teposcolula in Oaxaca, open chapels allowed the friars to conduct Mass outside before great crowds of the newly baptized gathered in the atrium. Many historians have noted how the open chapel allowed friars to say Mass before great crowds, far more people than could have ever squeezed into the modest interiors of the early churches. But as we have seen, since native Mexicans were accustomed to worshipping their gods outdoors, hearing Mass conducted from the open chapel helped make the new religion and its figures—the Father, Son, Holy Spirit, Mary, and the saints—easier to accept.

Within the sixteenth-century churches and convents, the friars often commissioned Native American painters to execute extensive mural programs on the walls of the nave and around the hallways of the cloister. They adopted the wall painting since it was relatively cheap in comparison with importing sculptures or canvases from Europe. During the early colonial era, few pictorial religious articles could be found in New Spain and were mostly limited to illustrated books like Bibles and missals. As mentioned previously, wall painting was well established in Precolumbian times and conveyed important political and religious messages. The friars used the paintings to teach Catholic doctrine to small groups of Native Americans. So we find, for example, the seven sacraments—Baptism, Confirmation, Matrimony, Eucharist, Penance, Anointing of the Sick, and Holy Orders—depicted on the convent walls at Tzintzuntzan, Michoacan. Other more spectacular cases include the mouth of Hell, depicted inside the open chapel at Actopan, Hidalgo, and the battle between Precolumbian Eagle and Jaguar knights, depicted on the walls of the Augustinian convent at Ixmiquilpan, also in the state of Hidalgo.

Few European painters worked in Mexico before the 1570s, and fewer still were wall painters. So the friars relied on ateliers of Native American wall painters who were instructed what to paint, and sometimes they

Murals at the Church of Ixmiquilpan, Hidalgo, Mexico, c. 1550. In the decades after the Conquest, the Spanish friars employed Indian artists to paint murals on the blank walls of newly built churches and cloisters. Scenes drawn from the Bible and Catholic doctrine served as didactic devices for Indian converts. The murals of the Augustinian monastery at Ixmiquilpan are a curious mix of Precolumbian and European imagery, with ancient Mexican warriors, European centaurs, and other late-medieval motifs.

worked from prints in religious books. As many researchers have noted, these Native American painters of the mid-sixteenth century often inserted Precolumbian imagery into their ostensibly Catholic murals. They also continued to render their scenes in Precolumbian styles completely lacking in modeling, perspective, and other features of European Renaissance painting. The finished works often resembled both sixteenth-century European prints and Precolumbian Mexican codices, the manuscripts used by the Aztecs and their neighbors.

Aside from religious establishments, many distinctly new-world solutions also developed in domestic architecture during the Spanish colonial era. Although Mexico's humblest inhabitants continued to live in the ancient thatched huts they had built since time immemorial, the middle and upper classes built sumptuous country haciendas and urban palaces. The hacienda, or country ranch, developed soon after the Conquest as the Spanish built estates near their rural farms and factories. Haciendas in central Mexico, like San Gabriel, Morelos, tended to produce sugar; whereas in both the northern and southern states, haciendas focused on cattle production. By the end of the 1850s, Yucatán haciendas specialized in producing sisal—hemp cordage used for nautical ropes and in agricultural harvesting.

The earliest Mexican haciendas were built during an era when Native American revolt and unrest in the countryside were real threats to the well-being of the hacienda owner, his family, and staff. Thus, many early hacienda owners built their ranches in such a way that they could be defended, with gates, towers, thick walls with parapets, and few windows. These haciendas resemble medieval Spanish castles, which present nearly blank faces to the exterior world and shelter a rich life of courtyards and arcades within.

With a few exceptions, the Mexican countryside settled down by the seventeenth century; much hacienda architecture continued to focus inward, becoming a way of life. And even as late as the early nineteenth century, some sections of New Spain remained very much on the frontier, with all of its dangers of Native

American raids and highwaymen. At the farthest reaches of the empire, in New Mexico, fortress ranches like the Martínez Hacienda in Taos were built as late as the end of the eighteenth century.

Hacienda Katanchel, Yucatán, Mexico, nineteenth century. Colonial Mexican haciendas were self-contained systems that produced everything needed for daily life, as well as cash crops such as cattle, sugar cane, and other agricultural products. Katanchel and other Yucatán haciendas began as cattle ranches, then switched to the extremely lucrative *henequén,* or sisal, after 1850. *Henequén* profits allowed Yucatán's hacienda owners to create grandiose architectural fantasies combining Moorish arches and draperies with other historical styles of European architecture.

Elsewhere in Mexico, late colonial haciendas gradually incorporated features better suited to life in the tropics than for defense from external threats. *Hacendados* began to build arcades and comfortable porches on the fronts of their ranch homes. These porches were ideally suited to the climate, and shielded the occupants from both rain and sun. During most of the colonial period and even much of the nineteenth century, Mexico's country haciendas were built throughout the countryside and not close to other estates, rather like the antebellum estates of the American South. Although there were Spanish and Moorish precedents for formal gardens, Mexican haciendas had no ornamental plantings until long after independence, when French landscape architecture began influencing home design.

Life in Mexico's cities during the colonial period also led to inward-turning dwellings, ranging from modest apartment blocks to the vast palaces of the nobility. In general, these

Montejo Palace, Mérida, Yucatán, c. 1550. Twenty years after the fall of the Aztec, Francisco Montejo led the Spanish forces that conquered the Maya of Yucatán. Unlike the country haciendas, this is an urban palace, with a façade unornamented except for the doorway, which features the Montejo family crest placed in a Renaissance-inspired architectural setting. As at Ixmiquilpan, Indian sculptors executed the Montejo Palace doorway in a mixture of Precolumbian and late-medieval styles.

structures, whether in urban or rural settings, were built to be defensible, with high walls, parapets, gates, and few entrances. Some homes of the early colonial period were decorated with wall paintings, like the churches and convents described above. In Puebla, the Casa del Dean has an extensive mural cycle showing allegorical figures of the liberal arts, derived almost certainly from book illustrations but painted by Native American artists. Few urban palaces of the sixteenth and seventeenth century survive, however, particularly in Mexico City, where periodic floods inundated the streets and in 1610 caused the entire downtown to sink deep into the muck that underlay the old Aztec capital.

A few examples of early colonial palaces can be found outside central Mexico, such as Casa de Montejo on the main square in Mérida, Yucatán. Like the religious establishments of the day, the Montejo Palace turns a blank face to the street; its only ornament is in the stone window frames and the important sculpture on the main gate. The latter shows both Gothic- and Renaissance-inspired details, the Montejo family arms, and grotesque images of Native Americans being crushed by the Spanish conquistadores. But Yucatán's Maya Native Americans were not subjugated so easily. After a bloody revolt in 1547, there were sporadic incidents throughout the colonial era and after, culminating in 1847 with the decades-long Caste War.

By the eighteenth century, the silver boom led to wholesale urban renewal in many of Mexico's cities, especially Morelia, Guadalajara, Puebla, and the capital. Many well-preserved palaces from the last century of

Metropolitan Cathedral, Mexico City. Immediately after the conquest of Mexico in 1521, the Spanish began to build churches atop Precolumbian temples, including the cathedral on the main square in Mexico City, which was built on top of the Aztec temple of the deity Quetzalcoatl and the ballcourt. The massive cathedral now dominates the central plaza of Mexico. Construction began in the 1560s and was finished in the early nineteenth century, after Mexican independence from Spain.

colonial rule can be found in central Mexico, like the palace of the Counts of Santiago y Calimaya in the capital. Modeled both on religious convents and Mediterranean prototypes stretching back to medieval Spain and Renaissance Italy, Mexico's urban palaces usually feature two or three stories of rooms organized around courtyards.

By the eighteenth century, Mexico City was the largest city in the Western Hemisphere, and the area around the Zócalo, the central square, was completely urbanized. The only open spaces downtown were the orchards and gardens of the monasteries and Alameda Park, at

this time still at the city's edge. Downtown, the administrative offices, churches, and palaces occupied complete blocks, and presented blank, seemingly forbidding façades to the streets. But the streets of the capital in the colonial period were alternately dusty or muddy, and were filled with filth and nefarious characters that contemporary writers called *léperos*. The famous *léperos* were just the city's poor, but the architecture was so forbidding on the outside that they might as well have been lepers. Many canals still crisscrossed the city during this period, vestiges of the Aztec city the conquistadors called the Venice of the New World. The canals were clean during Aztec times; but like in Venice, they were open sewers during the colonial era. Given all of the above factors, it is perhaps not surprising that the great urban palaces should turn a blank face to the streets.

Sagrario, Mexico City. The Sacristy to the cathedral's right was designed by Lorenzo Rodríguez and built from 1749 to 1768, and was the first example of the ultrabaroque style that became so popular in the New World.

Beginning in the seventeenth century and continuing until about 1800, the baroque style dominated Mexican art, literature, and architecture. Architects in New Spain created what has been called the *churrigueresque,* or ultra-baroque, style, characterized by a near-complete dissolution of building façades and interior decorative schemes in ornamentation. In church architecture, the best example of the Mexican ultrabaroque is also the first one built, the Metropolitan Sacristy, designed by Lorenzo Rodríguez and built next to the Mexico City Cathedral between 1749 and 1768. The Sacristy has an incredible accumulation of decorative elements that perforate the façade columns. In the Sacristy, Mexican architects first used the *estípite* column on an exterior façade. Unlike regular columns, *estípites* often have trapezoidal profiles and swell at the center, negating the illusion that they support weight. Many authors have noted that Mexican baroque church façades and the closely related form, the altar screens, seem to be applied like confectionery creations rather than solid architecture.

Life in baroque Mexican cities was filled with color, as builders continued to use red *tezontle* stone, and yellow *chiluca* for window and door frames. The resulting red-and-cream color scheme was unique to Mexico. Building exteriors were also decorated with colorful tiles called *azulejos,* found on scores of church domes in the city of Puebla. In Mexico City, the famous Casa de los Azulejos was built for the Counts of the Valle de Orizaba and was updated in the eighteenth century, with outside walls completely covered in blue tiles. This kind of tilework is just one of the many aspects of Mexican design that owes its origin to Spain's

Casa de los Azulejos, Mexico City, eighteenth century. This colonial urban palace was named after its exterior of blue and white *azulejos,* or tiles. Built for the Counts of the Valle de Orizaba, the Azulejo Palace is a good example of how Mexico's silver-rich nobles rebuilt the capital city in the eighteenth century. The Spanish adopted tiles from the Moors of southern Spain and north Africa. This kind of exterior tilework is typical of the region of the Mexican city of Puebla, where this family originated. Colonial Mexicans, like their Precolumbian ancestors, also decorated the exterior façades of their homes with bright colors.

Islamic history. Moorish-derived crafts and design elements, called *mudejar,* appeared everywhere in colonial Mexico, from the ceiling of the first Mexico City cathedral to the pointed arches and ornamental woodwork screens of urban palaces.

Yet despite the fantastic façades, altar screens, and tilework exteriors, baroque exuberance in colonial Mexico did not extend to either church plans or domestic design. With a handful of exceptions, there are no new-world equivalents of the undulating walls of

Borromini's San Carlo Alle Quattro Fontane in Rome (1638–41). Religious and domestic building plans remained conservative. Instead, we find the baroque expressed in decorative programs applied to building façades, especially around gates and portals. Otherwise, Mexico's nobility continued to build the same boxlike courtyard homes adapted from religious cloisters and Mediterranean palaces as they had in the preceding centuries.

Although the baroque style endured in Mexico longer than it did in Spain or Europe, its influence began to wane by the last decades of the eighteenth century. Enlightenment-era thought affected Mexican architecture primarily through the vehicle of neoclassicism. The Valencian sculptor and architect Manuel Tolsá inaugurated the Mexican neoclassical era when he arrived in 1791 to direct the sculpture program at San Carlos Academy, the official art school of colonial New Spain. Over thirty years, Tolsá completed many commissions in the neoclassical style, including the Caballito, the equestrian statue of King Charles IV, and the high altar for the Cathedral of Puebla. His reputation in architecture rests chiefly upon the School of Mines or "Palacio de Mineria" in Mexico City (1797–1813) and the Hospicio Cabañas in Guadalajara (1805). With these structures, Mexico shed baroque ornament and began building with clean façades and interiors. Tolsá's Hospicio Cabañas was constructed for an orphanage, and its church is now most famous for José Clemente Orozco's murals. But the structure caused a sensation in the early nineteenth century with its unornamented interior and façade free of baroque ornaments and *estípite* columns.

Manuel Tolsá, Palacio de Mineria, Mexico City, 1797–1813. Spanish architect Manuel Tolsá introduced French neoclassical style to Mexico at the end of the colonial period. This structure includes elements like columns, pediments, balustrades, rustication on the lowest level, and a clearly organized façade. Tolsá's restrained and highly structured style was in marked contrast to the exuberance of the Mexican ultrabaroque.

Among the homes Tolsá designed for the colonial elites of Mexico, the best preserved is the Palace of the Marqués de Buenavista, now the San Carlos Museum. Built in the early nineteenth century, the palace is a classic Mexican two-story courtyard home, occupying an entire block near Alameda Park in Mexico City. In some ways, the Buenavista Palace is conservative, with arcades fronting rooms on each floor. But the blocky exterior of the building conceals an unusual oval-shaped central courtyard. Like Tolsá's churches and his School of Mines, the Buenavista Palace has none of the baroque ornamentation of the previous century.

Manuel Tolsá, *Caballito.* An equestrian portrait of Charles IV, Mexico City, 1803. Although Tolsá designed this sculpture as the centerpiece of the Zócalo, it is now in front of the National Art Museum.

After Tolsá's death in 1816, Mexican architecture entered an extended period of contact with European styles that followed neoclassicism. Mexican elites and intellectuals looked to Europe—especially France—rather than to the United States for the latest styles of music, literature, art, and architecture. Mexico gained independence from Spain in 1821 and began a half-century of political upheaval, with four foreign invasions, two emperors, and fifty-seven regimes in fifty-five years. Mexico began to settle in 1876, when Porfirio Díaz began his thirty-five-year presidency. Díaz is widely remembered for his economic development programs that brought some sectors of the economy near to First World levels. Many Mexicans consider Díaz a traitor to the nation, and denounce his sale of many natural resources and industries to foreigners. But despite Don Porfirio's iron fist, Mexico made important contributions in art and architecture during the last quarter of the nineteenth century. Mexico leaped forward during the Díaz era,

and all the economic growth created vast fortunes for such families as the Maderos of Coahuila and the Terrazas and Creel clans of Chihuahua. Luis Terrazas once offered to pay off Mexico's national debt. Mexico's new wealth led to a building boom in both public and private sectors.

Of all the European styles favored in Porfirian Mexico, the French École des Beaux-Arts proved most influential. For the first time, Mexican homes in the later nineteenth century were designed with open façades, yards, and gardens. Although, this trend began in the mid-1860s when the Emperor Maximilian

Chapultepec Castle, Mexico City. In Precolumbian times, Chapultepec Hill was the center of the Aztec emperor's private park. During the colonial era, the viceroys built a fort on the hill's rocky summit. Since then, the castle has served as a military academy, the presidential residence, and now the National History Museum. The present structure was renovated by Mexico's Emperor Maximilian of Habsburg in the 1860s and later embellished by President Porfirio Díaz in the 1880s. Both Maximilian and Díaz brought contemporary French design and taste to Mexico and the castle reflects their desire to be in tune with European styles.

established the Avenida de la Reforma, connecting the Alameda Park and Chapultepec Castle grounds with a broad avenue of trees and beautiful homes consciously modeled on the efforts of Baron Haussmann in the Paris of Napoleon III. Since Mexico City's Reforma is now densely urbanized and packed with tall office buildings, we must leave the capital to see more intact neighborhoods of Díaz-era homes. The Paseo de Montejo in Mérida, Yucatán, was consciously modeled in 1902 on French boulevards and also on the Paseo de la Reforma. All along the Paseo can still be found turn-of-the-century palaces built with fortunes earned in the *henequén* trade. The Palacio Cantón, now the Mérida Archaeological Museum, is perhaps the best preserved of the Mérida palaces. Its exterior is a classic example of Beaux-Arts architecture, complete with a heavily ornamented upper façade, rusticated lower floor, and mansard roof, all accented with modeled-stucco sculpture. Inside, the palace makes a grand impression with Italian marble walls and floors; the home also boasted the first elevator on the Yucatán Peninsula. The Cantón Palace and other French-inspired homes in Mexico made a conscious break from the inward-turning architecture of the colonial era. Many feature wide lawns, ornamental gardens, and a generally open impression. The life of the family within is no longer hidden from the street. We find instead large banks of windows in impressive façades set back from the street.

## FUNCTIONALISM OR TRADITION: TWENTIETH-CENTURY MEXICAN ARCHITECTURE

Porfirio Díaz's regime crumbled in 1910, when his usual trick of fixing the outcome of presidential elections led to the start of an armed rebellion called by Francisco Madero, a wealthy hacienda owner from northern Mexico. Madero was the anti-reelectionist party candidate in the 1910 election. Regional strongmen throughout Mexico heeded Madero's call for revolution, and soon much of the nation was in

Diego Rivera, murals in the National Palace, Mexico City. Beginning in 1929, Diego Rivera painted one of the stairwells and an upstairs hallway with a vast panorama of Mexican history, from the Precolumbian Aztecs to the conquest, colonial era, independence, the Mexican-American War, the Porfirio Díaz era, the Mexican Revolution, and Rivera's vision of the future. He drew inspiration from ancient Mexican painted walls and those of the colony, and even employed some ancient technologies, like mixing cactus juice with his pigments. Like those earlier mural traditions, Rivera's paintings served a didactic function in addition to being decorative.

an uproar. Díaz resigned the presidency in 1911 and departed for Paris in exile, leaving Mexico to Madero. But the new president found that, once loosed, the revolutionary forces were difficult to rein in. Reactionary forces murdered Madero in 1913 and there followed seven years of chaos and destruction as the armies and generals such as Pancho Villa, Emiliano Zapata, and Venustiano Carranza fought for control of Mexico. The violence ended finally in 1920 with the inauguration of the Álvaro Obregón administration, led by one of the few generals left standing after the civil war.

After the revolution in the 1920s and 1930s, Mexico's leaders were quick to take all steps necessary to distance themselves from any connection to the disgraced Díaz regime. Like other revolutionary regimes, Mexico's leaders realized that art and architecture could play key roles in promoting the idea of a new nation. The Mexican muralist movement was by far the most important product of the revolutionary cultural policy. Inaugurated in 1922 by Education Minister José Vasconcelos, the muralist program commissioned vast public artworks on nationalistic themes from Diego Rivera, José Clemente Orozco, David Alfaro Siqueiros, and others. Rivera's murals presented both the clearest condemnation of the Díaz regime and the most unquestioning praise of the revolutionary generals and regime. In 1929, he began his most famous cycle of murals at the National Palace in Mexico City. They show the history of Mexico, from the Precolumbian Aztecs to the Colony, through the nineteenth century, the Díaz regime, and the revolution, ending with the prediction of a Marxist-Leninist paradise of workers for the future.

Adamo Boari and Federico Mariscal, Palace of Fine Arts, Mexico City, 1934. The Palace of Fine Arts was begun during the long presidency of Porfirio Díaz, and is an excellent example of French Beaux-Arts design. The Mexican Revolution interrupted its construction, and the palace was not completed until 1934. By this time, new design architect Mariscal added many art deco and art nouveau details on the interior, such as a glass stage curtain designed by Tiffany with a scene of the volcanoes of the Valley of Mexico. Today the palace is best known for its murals by Diego Rivera, David Alfaro Siqueiros, and José Clemente Orozco.

Rivera's murals formed part of a larger discourse on nationalism, art, and culture in postrevolutionary Mexico. Even before the revolution, Mexican artists and architects wondered if there was such a thing as a "Mexican style." After 1920, there was a political imperative to discover and promote Mexican national culture. Artists like Rivera espoused *indigenismo,* a theoretical stance glorifying the unique role of both the Precolumbian past and the living Native Americans in building Mexico's future. Others, like the painter Rufino Tamayo, preferred to be known as a modern artist rather than a modern Mexican artist. But for both critics and the public at large, "Mexican art" meant folk art on the one hand and the Mexican muralist movement on the other.

Le Corbusier, Villa Savoy, Poissy sur Seine, France, 1929. Le Corbusier was the genius of the International style, one of the dominant styles of twentieth-century modernist architecture. His architecture was a reaction against what he perceived as the superficial aspects of the art deco and art nouveau styles. Villa Savoy is a classic Le Corbusier design, with its clean lines, lack of interior or exterior ornament, use of industrial materials, and monochrome approach. All of these characteristics were influential in Mexico.

At least initially, the Mexican Revolution failed to yield a nationalistic architecture to match the muralist movement. Little construction dates from the chaotic years between 1910 and about 1925. The new revolutionary governments finished some Díaz-era public buildings, like the Palace of Fine Arts, begun as a stupendous Beaux-Arts and art nouveau theater designed by Adamo Boari in the last years of the *ancien régime.* The palace was finally completed in 1934, with many new details added in the art deco style by Federico Mariscal, including a glass curtain by Tiffany and architectural details in Maya and Aztec art deco. In the 1930s and after, the palace became a kind of shrine to the Mexican muralists, with works by Rivera, Orozco, Siqueiros, and Tamayo. For the palace, Rivera re-created the mural *Man at the*

*Crossroads,* which was destroyed in 1933 at Rockefeller Center, New York, following a dispute between the artist and the Rockefeller family.

Besides art deco, architecture in Mexico after the revolution was dominated by nationalistic and such socially oriented projects as hospitals, clinics, and the monument to the revolution. Architects like José Villagrán García, Carlos Obregón Santacilia, and Enrique Yáñez used their skills to demonstrate that Mexico could show her clean break with the past, even in architecture. Although these designers made important contributions to twentieth-century Mexican architecture, artists Juan O'Gorman and Mathias Goeritz proved more influential in moving the idiom to the next level. As a young man, O'Gorman discovered the writings of the influential French architect Le Corbusier and was impressed by the concepts of functionalism, rationalism, and architectural plasticity. He studied architecture and painting

Juan O'Gorman. Connected homes for Diego Rivera and Frida Kahlo, Mexico City, 1929–30. Juan O'Gorman brought the styles of Le Corbusier and the Bauhaus to Mexico. Emblematic of the troubled relationship between Diego Rivera and his wife Frida Kahlo, O'Gorman designed side-by-side homes and studios connected by a bridge.

at the National University of Mexico under Villagrán and Guillermo Zárraga. At the university, his professors further exposed him to the latest in European functionalist design theory, including the latest works of Le Corbusier and the theory and practice of the Bauhaus.

O'Gorman is best known in Mexico as the promoter of the ideas of Le Corbusier and what would later be called the International style. Le Corbusier himself was active in Latin America, especially in South America, but not in Mexico. O'Gorman brought his theories to the land of Montezuma. As the chief architect of the education ministry, he devised a new approach to building schools based on a module that could be replicated and expanded to fit any need. Between 1933 and 1934, O'Gorman renovated thirty-three schools and built twenty more, and his module departed from the old colonial model of schools based on the religious cloister. O'Gorman's domestic projects proved more influential for the history of home design in Mexico. His homes for Diego Rivera and Frida Kahlo (1929–30) and the one he designed for himself (1931–32) were excellent examples of early functionalism, with their emphasis on a low boxy feel, industrial building materials, clean-lined windows, and steel moldings. With its raking skylights and banks of windows, the Rivera home is very reminiscent of the Amédée Ozenfant Studio, designed in 1922 by Le Corbusier and Pierre Jeanneret. Like his models, Le Corbusier's Villa Savoy and the buildings of the Bauhaus itself, O'Gorman's designs for homes and schools are colorless and devoid of exterior ornament. He promoted functionalism in Mexico as the architectural style that matched the new socially oriented post-revolutionary regime.

In addition to his role as promoter of modernism in Mexican architecture, O'Gorman also enjoyed a long career as a painter and muralist. He was active in the plastic integration movement of the 1950s, which aimed to integrate painting and sculpture with architecture and urban planning. His best-known work in this arena was the mosaic mural he executed over 4,000 square meters of all four exterior walls of the Main Library at the National University in Mexico City (1948–50). Unlike his architecture, O'Gorman's murals were characterized by bright colors and motifs drawn from the Precolumbian past. In a way, O'Gorman's murals extended the life of the muralist movement, with its focus on

Mathias Goeritz and Luis Barragán, Satélite Towers, Mexico City, 1957. These towers marked the entrance to Satellite City, a new development on the outskirts of Mexico City in the late 1950s. Constructed of reinforced concrete and painted red, yellow, and white, the towers rise between 100 and 165 feet. Although the towers are not buildings in the traditional sense, functioning more like sculpture, they remain among the most important legacies of Mexican modernism.

renovating and discovering new roles for Mexico's Precolumbian past.

Aside from O'Gorman, Mathias Goeritz was the other principal promoter of European functionalism in Mexican architecture. After studying philosophy and art history in Berlin, Goeritz spent the 1940s as an arts educator in Spain. He moved to Mexico in 1949 and taught design at the University of Guadalajara and later in Mexico City. His most influential period began in 1951, when he founded the Museo Experimental El Eco in the capital and installed his own sculptures in its courtyard. To celebrate the museum opening, Goeritz published the manifesto *Arquitectura emocional,* which promoted organic architecture and a unique approach to space design. Later in the 1950s, Goeritz collaborated with Luis Barragán on several important projects, including the development of the Pedregal. But Goeritz's most visible legacy is the Satélite Towers, created with Barragán in 1957. Ciudad Satélite was a northern suburb of Mexico City, now surrounded by the metropolis. Goeritz and his friend Barragán designed six blank concrete towers, each between 100 and 165 feet in height, painted yellow, red, and white.

Luis Barragán, perhaps the most influential Mexican architect, adapted the clean lines of European functionalism to the climate and color of Mexico, and synthesized native Mexican and international trends in architecture. Barragán was a native of Guadalajara and studied engineering at the university there in the early 1920s. Over the next ten years, he traveled to the United States and Europe twice, where his travels exposed him not only to the traditional Moorish-inspired Spanish architec-

ture of square homes closed to the outside, with courtyards and gardens within, but also to the most advanced modernist architectural theory. He attended Le Corbusier's lectures in Paris in 1932, and met French landscape architect Ferdinand Bac, author of a work on integrating nature and architecture called *Jardins Enchantés* (1925). Back in Mexico during the 1930s, Barragán promoted the

Luis Barragán. Barragán House, Tacubaya, Mexico City. 1947-1948. In the study is one of Barragán's signature "floating" stairways. This serves both a functional and decorative purpose.

Corbusian International style as an alternative to the sentimental California mission–style homes advocated soon after the revolution by José Vasconcelos as the new national style.

With Juan O'Gorman, Barragán promoted the use of industrial materials, clean lines, and exterior façades free of ornament. He built dozens of homes and some apartment buildings during the 1930s, most in styles derived from Le Corbusier.

Luis Barragán, Barragán House, Tacubaya, Mexico City, 1947–1948. View of the house from the garden shows Barragán's use of color, geometry, and exposed lava rock.

Barragán changed both his personal style and the direction of his career in 1944, when he purchased 865 acres in Mexico City's Pedregal with the help of a private investor. The Pedregal was a desolate rough lava flow on Mexico City's south side near the colonial-era neighborhood of San Angel. Up to this time, few people lived on the Pedregal, and most considered it impossible to develop. Barragán accepted the challenge and built the Parque Residencial Jardines del Pedregal de San Angel (1945–50), a housing development organized on the principle of integrating site and architecture. Barragán's designs for the Pedregal are masterful essays in blending architecture with landscape fea-

tures, and betray his interest in the designs of Frank Lloyd Wright.

After the Pedregal development, Barragán's best known projects were his own home, the equestrian estates of Las Arboledas (1958–61) and San Cristóbal at Los Clubes (1968). His home in Tacubaya (1947–48), Mexico City, is a sensitive combination of courtyards, gardens, and water features, all removed from the street by high walls. Barragán disliked the giant plate-glass windows made popular by Mies van der Rohe, Philip Johnson, and other modernist architects. He thought they were better suited to sports arenas, where spectators needed vast windows to see the action outside. In contrast, Barragán saw the home as a sanctuary, where it was critical to preserve a sense of the private and mysterious. His homes usually had thick walls, small windows, and intimate spaces built on a human scale. In this sense his work continued the Mexican colonial approach to homes, with their nondescript street façades and inward-turning focus. Barragán oftentimes designed dramatic staircases inside the homes that functioned as active design elements, not the simple utilitarian means of ascending to the upper story. In his own home, he cantilevered one stairway from the study wall, with no railing. Another ascends from the front door to a somewhat mysterious darkened landing, seemingly lit by the gold leaf of a Mathias Goeritz painting.

Yet one cannot escape the influence of twentieth-century architecture in the homes of Barragán. He assembled his designs from the simplest geometric shapes, perhaps derived ultimately from cubism and, later, abstract art. Barragán homes seem like assemblages of cubes and

Luis Barragán, Barragán House, Tacubaya, Mexico City, 1947–48. Stairs play both a practical and decorative role in a Barragán home, continuing the ancient Mexican emphasis on stairways as active design elements. The golden painting on the stairwell is by Mathias Goeritz, a friend and collaborator of Barragán's.

other basic volumetric forms, with sharp edges, a complete lack of ornamental moldings and other features designed to warm the icy cold of geometric abstraction. But a Barragán home escapes the chill feel of a Le Corbusier home—or even one by Juan O'Gorman—by its addition of bright color. Barragán used color as an active design element along with his signature geometric volumes.

As mentioned previously, color played a key role in Mexican architecture and design in both Precolumbian and colonial eras; throughout

rural Mexico today, many small villages are a riot of color, with what seems like every other house and building painted another bright color. Barragán continued that Mexican tradition and brought color to the idiom of modern architecture. His own home has walls of bright pink and yellow; he often used purples, reds, and blues, not simply as accent colors but as main colors for large sections of walls, both inside and out.

Barragán's use of color is perhaps the key to understanding why the great Mexican writer Octavio Paz described him as modern but not

Luis Barragán, Barragán House, Tacubaya, Mexico City, 1947–48. During the late 1940s, Barragán developed his signature style, with its clean modernist line, bright colors, and lack of ornamentation. He conceived of his homes as refuges from the bustle of urban life, and they often feature thick privacy walls, small windows to the street, gardens, fountains, and other details that lend a sense of tranquility.

a modernist. Important strands of the narrative of twentieth-century Euro-American modernism concerned themselves with draining both color and figuration from art and architecture. Both were considered distractions from the heroic drive toward abstraction and the future. Le Corbusier and the Bauhaus created entire schools of monochrome architecture. Barragán adapted significant aspects of the modernist language but corrupted them with color. Diego Rivera suffered the same criticism for never being able to drop the color from the fine cubist-style canvases he painted while living for more than a decade in Paris in the early twentieth century. He painted the brightly colored *Zapatista Landscape—The Guerrilla* (1915) at the same time and place, and in the same style as Picasso and Braque's greatest synthetic cubist works. But Picasso and Braque dropped color from their works, Rivera never could.

Barragán was a devout Catholic; further, he adopted a mystical attitude toward the built environment. He felt that modern people were dislocated from the landscape and its mythical and religious qualities. Architecture—what he called *arquitectura emocional*—could reforge humanity's link with the spiritual. Barragán's approach and his architecture were far from the cold functionalism we usually associate with the structures of Le Corbusier, the Bauhaus, or Mies van der Rohe. His was more like the spiritualism that underlays the hard-edged abstraction of Piet Mondrian, or the abstract expressionism of Barnett Newman and Mark Rothko. Barragán designed his homes as private refuges, configured to yield an almost Zen-like solitude.

## HIJOS DE LA TRADICIÓN (SONS OF THE TRADITION): MEXICO 1980s–1990s

Luis Barragán was the most influential architect to emerge out of the building boom in post–World War II Mexico. Dozens of other architects reached their mature styles during this period, including Mario Pani, Pedro Ramírez Vásquez, Rafael Mijares, Félix Candela, Enrique Yáñez, Enrique del Moral, Salvador Ortega Flores, Augusto Pérez Palacio, Augusto Alvarez, Juan Sordo Maldonado, and many others. Their reputations rest primarily upon large state-sponsored projects in Mexico City, like the new University City in the Pedregal (1948–52), where some sixty architects and artists, directed by Pani and del Moral, designed and executed a vast campus still

Pedro Ramírez Vásquez, Jorge Campuzano, and Rafael Mijares, courtyard of the National Museum of Anthropology, Mexico City, 1964. Ramírez Vásquez was one of the most prominent practitioners of the International style in Mexico. His best-known work is the great Museum of Anthropology, with its monumental concrete umbrella covering the central courtyard. This feature shades the court and functions as an upside-down fountain.

used today by more than 100,000 students. Pani also designed the Miguel Alemán housing complex (1949–50) in the capital, Ciudad Satélite (1957), and the Rectory building at the University (1951–52), with its library decorated by Juan O'Gorman. Generally, all of these architects worked in local varieties of modernism and the International style, with special emphasis on exploring the possibilities of industrial materials, especially cast concrete. For the National Museum of Anthropology (1964), Pedro Ramírez Vásquez designed a spectacular concrete umbrella that covers much of a huge interior courtyard. The umbrella also functions as a fountain, and Ramírez Vásquez placed bronze reliefs with Precolumbian motifs on its massive tree-like shaft.

The Mexican government continued as one of the major patrons of architecture through the 1960s, especially after the 1968 Tlatelolco massacre of student protesters by government troops. In the world of colossal commissions—like the Olympic stadiums and such skyscrapers as the Torre Latino Americano in Mexico City (1957)—there seemed little room for the intimate architecture promoted by Luis Barragán. Yet in spite of the vast scale of many of the most significant structures built after 1968, several distinct schools of domestic architecture developed. The senior members of the group treated in this book—Agustín Hernández, Abraham Zabludovsky, Teodoro González de León, and Ricardo Legorreta—began their practices during this turbulent period.

This book focuses on homes designed by Mexican architects primarily in the 1980s and

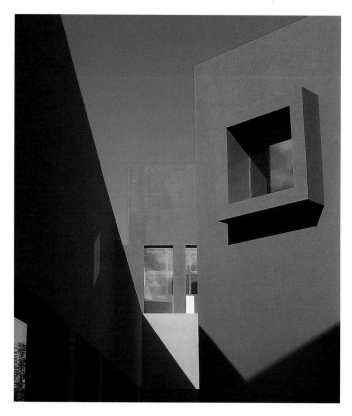

Legorreta + Legorreta, Visual Arts Center, College of Santa Fe, New Mexico, 1999. Ricardo Legorreta is one of the most prominent Mexican architects today. His work is known for its bright color and geometry. At the College of Santa Fe, he designed a complex of art buildings around courtyards with covered walkways that harken back to both the Precolumbian palaces of Teotihuacán and the cloisters of colonial Mexico.

1990s. All the architects presented also design large projects, like Legorreta's Visual Arts Center at the College of Santa Fe (1999), or the Colegio de México by González de León and Zabludovsky (1974–75). Although we present homes built for both urban and suburban settings—a mixture of city houses and weekend getaways—we do not address multifamily apartment buildings, large private country haciendas, or resort homes. The last is a specialized subgroup of Mexican architecture that builds homes using the *palapa,* or thatched roof, as a principal organizing element.

Recent and contemporary Mexican home designs fall into several general style categories. If asked about modern Mexican architecture, most interested laymen would mention the bright colors and geometric forms of Luis Barragán. After all, Barragán won the Pritzker Prize in 1980, architecture's highest honor, and his work has been influential to architects around the world. Barragán's architectural followers can be thought of as the colorists or as the traditionalists: they use color as an active design element combined with various aspects of modern architecture. Among the colorists, we present homes by Ricardo Legorreta, Jorge Alessio Robles, and José de Yturbe.

A second group of architects presented here might be thought of as eclectics. The homes of Agustín Hernández and José Luis Esquerra represent highly personal visions of architectural space, mass, and volume. Hernández's own home and his architectural studio are perched on steep hillsides in Mexico City's Lomas District, and convey a futuristic vision with their stark geometry, bold placement, and innovative use of materials. At the other end of the geometric perspective, Esquerra designs homes based on both organic forms and North African traditional architecture. His houses feel Mediterranean and subterranean at the same time, with their towers, curving parapets, and round windows.

The third group of Mexican architects continues working in a more international style descended from the modernism of Le Corbusier and O'Gorman. Among the purists or functionalists, we find homes designed by Abraham Zabludovsky, Teodoro González de León, Carlos Santos Maldonado, J. B.

Johnson, Félix Sánchez, Enrique Norten, and Isaac Broid. These architects tend to use industrial materials like concrete and brushed aluminum, with large banks of windows and almost no color. Their work participates in the latest trends of international postmodern architecture, and many of their projects would be equally at home in Amsterdam, Rome, or Mexico City.

This abbreviated summary of Mexican architecture outlines some of the cultural and historical forces that have helped shape one of the world's most vibrant traditions of contemporary design. As mentioned above, this book presents the work of only a handful of the many creative designers active in Mexico today. We could mention many other architects, including Billy Springall, Mario Schjetnan, Agustín Landa, Marisa Aja, Agusto Quijano, Ligia Vásquez, and others, whose work could not be included, but who we hope to present in future publications. Although many of our architects also design large public buildings, we have chosen to present only homes, and only projects that have actually been completed. We have followed the wishes of the architects by referring to many projects by the initials of the owners, as in Enrique Norten's R. R. House, or by nicknames, like Ricardo Legorreta's "Japan House."

Life in a home designed by one of the architects presented here is a constant feast of light, color, and texture. We hope this book introduces our readers to a rich architectural tradition close to home, and that they may perhaps gain design ideas, or even choose to have a Mexican architect design their home.

# COLORISTS

Mexico is a land of brilliant light and bright color. From Precolumbian times forward, Mexicans have painted the walls of their living spaces with bright colors. Streets in small-town Mexico are a feast for the eye, with home after home decorated in the brightest colors available, hues seemingly required by both the Mexican temperament and the clear blue sky. Responding to this tradition, Luis Barragán introduced color into the vocabulary of Mexican architecture beginning in the mid-twentieth century. Color in Barragán's houses functions as an active design element, as important as integration with the landscape, staircases, fountains, pools, and small windows. Barragán's famous Pedregal subdivision, designed in the 1950s and 1960s, offers a dramatic example of adapting design to setting, with homes placed over and around a large lava flow on the outskirts of Mexico City. He combined all of these features to express what he called an "emotional architecture."

Many Mexican architects after Barragán adopted his approach to both color and landscape integration. Indeed, no matter how one characterizes contemporary Mexican architecture, its practitioners across the stylistic spectrum show great sensitivity to the physical setting of their designs. They do not believe, as do some schools of modern Euro-American architecture, that the building alone makes the project. Mexico is a country of great contrasts in its landscape, from the jungles of Chiapas and Yucatán in the south to the cold high deserts of Chihuahua and Sonora in the north. This variety of landscape creates opportunities for very different types of houses. Of course, most Mexican architects also design homes in urban settings like Mexico City, where unusually shaped and densely urbanized lots can challenge even the most inventive architects.

The use of bright color characterizes the work of a large group of architects active in Mexico today. In this section, we present homes designed by three of Mexico's most prominent colorist architecture firms: Legorreta + Legorreta, Jorge Alessio Robles, and José de Yturbe. All adapted Barragán's interest in color as an integral design element.

# LEGORRETA + LEGORRETA

Legorreta + Legorreta is perhaps Mexico's most famous architectural firm, begun by Ricardo Legorreta thirty years ago and now joined by his son Victor Legorreta. The best-known student of Barragán, Ricardo Legorreta entered the Mexican architectural scene in the late 1960s with designs for both private homes and large public buildings. He adapted the idiom of Barragán—based on intimate spaces designed for modest private dwellings—to much larger commissions like the Camino Real Hotel in Mexico City (1968), the Cathedral in Managua, Nicaragua (1993), and the Visual Arts Center at the College of Santa Fe, New Mexico (1999). Legorreta has also designed private homes in Mexico, the United States, and Japan. In 2000, the American Institute of Architects recognized his contribution to world architecture with its gold medal, one of architecture's highest honors.

Legorreta is best known for his colors and his walls, used in a vigorous and expressive manner to seal the buildings from the street. Light and shadow, planned views, and water figure prominently in his designs. He uses spaces and shapes to create dramatic effects. His buildings and his clients should, in Legorreta's opinion, have an effect on each other. This approach is distinct from pure functionality, which tries to inhibit the user with a universal anonymous space. Unlike many Mexican architects who have achieved success, Legorreta still designs single-family homes.

The Japan House (2000), located on the edge of the sea south of Tokyo, is an example of Legorreta's site-specific talents. In this dramatic location, Legorreta uses the site to set a theme; it is a house with comfortable contra-dictions, a retreat open to the expanse of the sea. Water meets water as he sites a lap pool almost hanging off the house over the ocean. The tall white walls of the house change color with the weather, and the deep interior recesses offer refuge and warmth. The approach is through an open courtyard into the blue interior of a guard tower that leads into a large vaulted gallery, also blue, echoing the ocean. The terraces lead to the interior and make a strong connection with the landscape. There is a garage under the house and the mechanical features are hidden. This house fits well into the minimalist Japanese aesthetic but retains its Mexican character.

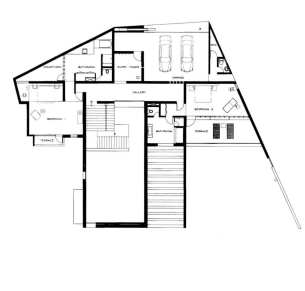

30

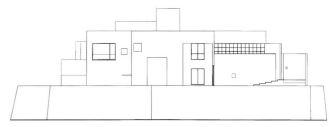

Page 28: Japan House, 2000. A brilliant blue gallery forms the backbone of the house, connecting the entry tower, two upstairs bedrooms, and the double-height dining and living rooms.

Above: South Elevation.

Opposite: Japan House. The ocean façade and patio. A lap pool marks the boundary between home and sea. Unlike many Legorreta houses, the Japan House is white on the outside, with bright colors inside. The color, water features, and landscaping lend the home a Zen aesthetic in keeping with the Japanese setting.

Left: Japan House. View from the living room into the dining area, with the blue gallery above and behind. The skylight and a basket-work light fixture hanging from the ceiling ensure the same light levels day and night. The circular mirrors on the pink wall reflect the sea from the picture window.

31

Opposite: Japan House. Lower-level living room, with view out to the lap pool and ocean. The light-colored décor of the interior contains typical Legorreta accents like the natural wood furniture and hand-blown glass balls. The couch backs up to the dining room table, hand-made of pine in Mexico.

Above, left: Japan House. View of the home from the ocean. The lap pool continues the water motif around the house so that it appears to float in a mysterious way. This façade has no transition from the house walls to the water of the lap pool, emphasizing the naturally dramatic setting at the edge of the sea.

Below, left: Japan House. Street façade, parking, and entry tower. The blank tower with vertical slot windows are Legorreta trademarks. With its moat-like lap toward the sea, and a stern and unornamented façade facing the street, this home emphasizes its function as a private sanctuary.

Page 34: Japan House. View from the gallery down into the dining room and living room. Carefully managed light fixtures, windows, and bright colors make the inside of the house appear to glow. The bright pink of the stairway and recessed lights are Legorreta trademarks.

Page 35: Japan House, 2000. The patio looks north out over the ocean near Tokyo. Legorreta homes share purity and an elegant use of geometric shapes.

Opposite: House of Fifteen Patios, Mexico City, 1996–98. Bathroom with a skylight covered with a wooden grid that softens and diffuses the light. Legorreta + Legorreta often paint skylights so that the natural sunlight diffuses the painted color throughout the room.

Above, left: House of Fifteen Patios. The entrance patio has several platforms with water features that create a peaceful environment.

Below, left: House of Fifteen Patios. The interior of this house is punctuated by fifteen patios, many with water features.

Opposite: House of Fifteen Patios. This large (12,500 sq. ft.) walled house in Mexico City's Lomas de Chapultepec neighborhood turns inward and away from the street.

Left: House of Fifteen Patios. Pink patio with ornamental palm trees and *equipal* furniture, a traditional Mexican leather-covered furniture.

# JORGE ALESSIO ROBLES

Jorge Alessio Robles graduated in 1977 from the Iberoamericana University in Mexico City, and obtained a graduate degree in urban design from the University of Pennsylvania in 1984. He worked for Ricardo Legorreta and is continuing the tradition of Barragán, using vibrant colors and light. These lend his spaces austerity and spatial richness simultaneously. In this way he is closer to Barragán, who was mainly interested in the home as a place of sanctuary. In his architecture, there are gridlike piercing elements derived from Moroccan privacy screens, first used by Barragán and certainly an important element for Legorreta. Alessio Robles uses these to soften the effect of a blank wall, to allow for ventilation, and create a checkered play of inside light.

Alessio Robles also incorporates water features: fountains and pools that catch the bright colors of the walls and cool the halls and patios. He uses glass walls and mixes these with much more traditional Mexican elements: tile roofs and artisan materials, tiles and stone. There are large boxlike elements, tall framing devices and industrial brick that are more functionalist than colorist. His color palette is typical of the colorists, rich and containing the range of Mexican colors—clear cobalt blue, chrome yellow, and strong shades of red, pink, salmon, and rose—colors that pierce the air and define the buildings. There are hanging stairs and square bookcases, as well as skywalks or bridges connecting buildings—common elements in colorist architecture. Low windows with almost secret views into gardens are often found in both colorist and functionalist architecture.

The house the architect designed for himself naturally contains most of the elements of this style. The house has a bright pink exterior and glass-brick windows that protrude outside the walls, letting in light but affording privacy, too. They punctuate the wall and act as small opaque balconies or window seats. Alessio Robles's library is a welcoming space lined with books, offering an inviting glimpse into the garden.

The Casa Diego y Mercedes Landa Los Encinos, in the state of Mexico, is another example of the architect's colorist architecture. The inside of the house features a bridge, suspended over the first floor, that joins two parts of the house. Along this wall there are small square openings for light and ventilation. There are skylights above that floor so the double-story space is filled with light.

Another house by Alessio Robles is Casa Mula in Jajalpa, in the state of Mexico. Built in 1998, it has several water features, including a spout of water falling into a stone box and a trough of water under a window, both cooling and soothing the outdoor areas of the house. These features add charm and lend a distinctly Mexican ambiance to the house.

Page 40: Casa Mulas, Jajalpa, Estado de Mexico, 1998. Mexican homes like the Mulas House often contain water features. This is one of the simplest and most effective, where a spout emerges from a wall painted in a favorite shade of blue.

Casa Mulas. In the home's patio, another water feature is sited directly below a window. The water slides off a sluice into and over a tile basin, then into a small catchment return.

44

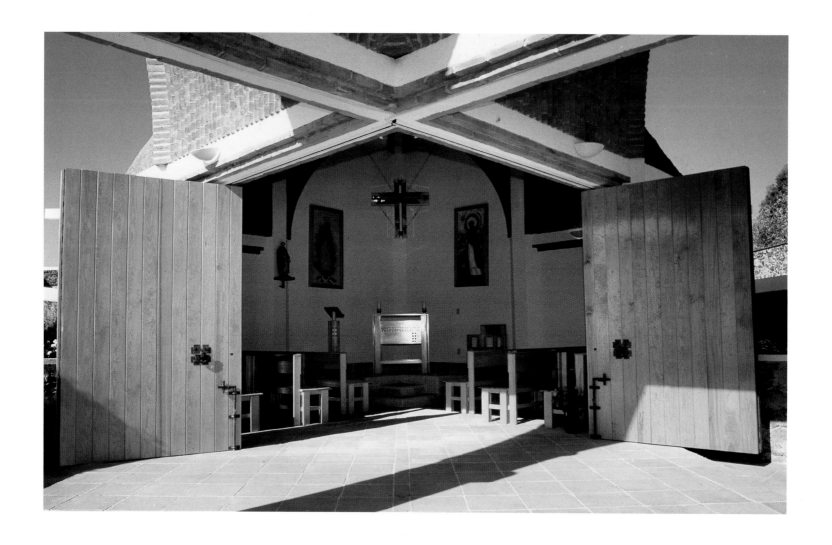

Chapel in Rancho Cerro Gordo, Polotitlan,
State of Mexico, 1999. With the doors open, this
small sanctuary resembles the open chapels of
sixteenth-century Mexico.

Page 44: Chapel in Rancho Cerro Gordo. An
ingenious system of brick vaults creates the roof of
this chapel.

Page 45: View of the back of the chapel. Twin
clerestories light the altar and alleviate the strict
geometry of the building.

Chapel in Rancho Cerro Gordo.
Large homes and country ranches in Mexico frequently contain private chapels. In this commission, the architect designed a new chapel for an
existing historic hacienda. Harkening back to early
colonial times, Alessio Robles placed a cross in
the atrium in front of the chapel. The materials
used in the construction are similar to those used
in the older parts of the ranch.

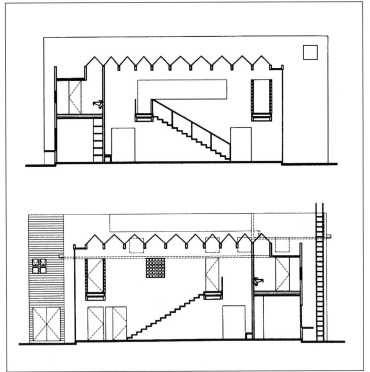

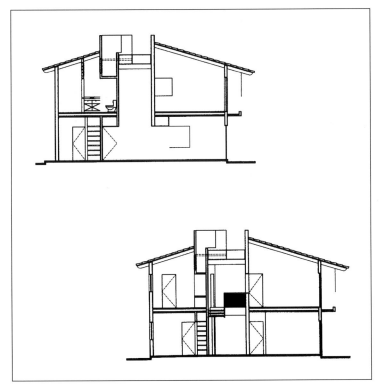

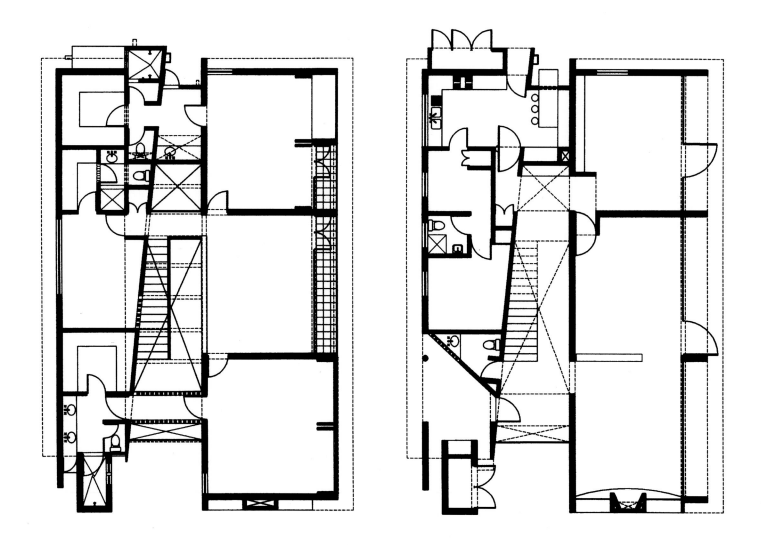

Page 48: Casa Diego y Mercedes Landa, Los Encinos, Estado de Mexico, 1996. This architect is known for his masterful use of brick. This house outside Mexico City sits back from the street and has a garden in front, setting it apart from most of the other homes in this book.

Page 49, top: Casa Diego y Mercedes Landa. The view from the second story through the central corridor shows the glass roofing elements and walkway, with a gridlike ventilation and privacy feature on the right wall.

Page 49, bottom: A central corridor in this house links the left and right sections, and contains a stairway and an upstairs walkway.

Above, left: Upper Floor, Casa Diego y Mercedes Landa.

Above, right: Lower Floor, Casa Diego y Mercedes Landa.

Above: Casa Ochoa. Shed roofs in combination with stricter geometric forms is a hallmark of Alessio Robles.

Page 52: Casa Ochoa, Jajalpa, Estado de Mexico, 1997. The central corridor of this house shows the seamless transition between inside and outside, a frequent characteristic of Mexican houses.

51

Page 53: Casa Alessio Robles, Mexico City, 1992. The architect's own house is organized around a hot pink and white interior patio. Here glass bricks allow in light while preserving privacy.

Opposite: Casa Alessio Robles. An upstairs patio combines color and geometry with a view of the garden below.

Right: Casa Alessio Robles. The hot pink color scheme continues inside the house, as in this library, where it is combined with natural wood floors, furniture, and window shutters.

# JOSÉ DE YTURBE

José de Yturbe is one of the better-known Mexican architects of the younger generation who employs color in the modernist mode. Like many of the other architects featured in this book, de Yturbe studied architecture at Mexico's Iberoamericana University. He quickly gained recognition for his bold use of color in the tradition of Barragán. Although de Yturbe has designed commercial projects like the Westin Regina Hotel (1995) in Los Cabos, Baja California (with Javier Sordo Maldonado), he is not known for gigantic corporate or public commissions. Instead, his practice focuses on private dwellings like the MG House, the El Sabino Country House, the SY Country House, and the House in Las Lomas.

De Yturbe designed the salmon pink MG House for a lush setting outside San José, Costa Rica (1994). The home is organized to take advantage of mountain views, with outdoor patios on all sides. In one patio, a raised circular pond with a semi-submerged concrete sphere lends a minimalist aspect. Walls with open sections surround the patio and come to a corner that seems to point to a cleft in the mountains behind the home. On the other side of the house, another terrace opens on a ver-

dant landscape of banana plants and other tropical greenery. But no wall separates this outdoor living room from nature. Instead, a swimming pool with an infinity edge seems to erase the boundary between the natural and the man-made.

Inside the MG House, de Yturbe continued the salmon color scheme found outside. The dining room uses bright colors, large windows, plants, and light-colored pine furniture to convey an overall warm and inviting impression.

De Yturbe's El Sabino Country House (1997) in Santa Maria Acatitlan, State of Mexico, is also constructed around patios with water features. These are concealed behind high walls painted orange and yellow. In the city these kinds of walls establish the privacy of the home within; but here in the countryside, de Yturbe pierced the walls with dramatic openings that create a sculptural effect. The home is entered through a pink patio with a stepped bank of maguey cactus on one side. Access to the house is through a cast-concrete door that pivots on a single cardinal hinge.

On the other side of the house, a shady porch opens on an even more dramatic patio. De Yturbe combined new and old technology in this courtyard, with the tile shed roof of the porch contrasting with the knife edge of the orange walls. The court also includes a large reflecting pool with a dramatic flying beam that ties the two halves of the home together.

Page 56: Casa in Las Lomas, Mexico City, 1995. The architect built this home mostly below street level in Mexico City's Las Lomas neighborhood. Giant maguey plants in the entrance are a tribute to the sun and sky.

Above, right: Casa in Las Lomas.
The architect coordinated the art so that it is in keeping with the home's scale, proportion and color scheme.

Right: Casa in Las Lomas.
A view into the circular library across the triangular reflecting pool. De Yturbe achieves integration with nature through windows on the lower floor that overlook the central courtyard.

Above: Casa in Las Lomas. The Lomas House faces south and is flooded with natural light throughout the day. Light and color play key roles in this house. The concrete lattice projects shadows inside the house onto the walls of a circular staircase.

Left: Casa in Las Lomas. De Yturbe's circular library provides a natural gathering place for the family.

Page 60: Casa in Las Lomas. The home's interior courtyard has a triangular shallow pool that continues the Islamic use of water features to cool and beautify spaces.

Page 61: Casa in Las Lomas. The triangular pool viewed from another angle provides the house with the soothing accompaniment of water.

Opposite: SY Country House, La Peña, Valle del Bravo, 1994. An infinity lap pool on the outside patio unites the lake and mountains with the house.

Left: SY Country House. A covered patio at the heart of the house contains a large fireplace that provides warmth against the chill of the lake.

Above: SY Country House. The stairway leads from the
covered patio to the bedroom level.

Above: SY Country House. This house is situated at the edge of a steep ravine, and was designed for the owners to enjoy beautiful vistas of the lake and mountains and make the outside an integral part of the house.

Right: El Sabino Country House, Santa Maria Acatitlan, State of Mexico, 1997. The pattern of the patio floor contrasts with the strong color of the wall and the pattern of the tile roof.

Below: El Sabino Country House. View from outside the house through a narrow channel to the larger pool in the central patio.

Above: El Sabino Country House.
Brilliantly colored high baffles
provide a glimpse of the
protected interior patio and
pool of this house.

67

Right: Floorplan of El Sabino
Country House.

Page 69: El Sabino Country House.
The house is organized around a
large central patio with a
reflecting pool spanned by a
colored beam.

Page 70: MG House. An infinity
pool with cast-concrete lounges
affords swimmers vistas of the lush
Costa Rican rain forest.

Page 71: MG House. De Yturbe
integrated the pool with indoor living spaces. A white curving path
leads past the pool and into the
house. On the second story a privacy grate echoes the window
below and lights an interior patio.

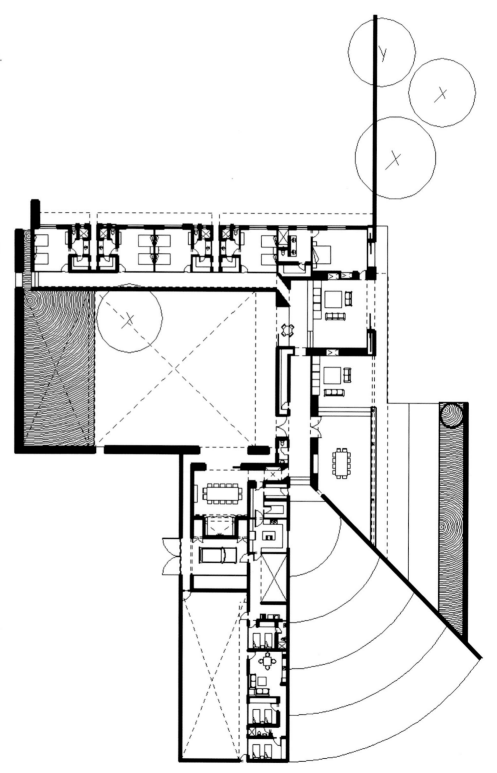

# PERSONAL VISIONS

In creative fields like the visual arts and architecture, every generation yields talents whose work cannot be characterized by terms like modern, functionalist, or postmodern. These individuals often seem far ahead of their time, and their innovative approaches provide wellsprings of inspiration for their contemporaries and followers alike. In the field of architecture, many unique spirits come to mind. The United States has Canadian Frank Gehry, with his famous Guggenheim Museum in Bilbao, Spain. Spain has Santiago Calatrava, designer of the City of the Arts in Valencia and the new Milwaukee Art Museum, and of course the heritage of Antonio Gaudí. Mexico has had its share of unique twentieth-century architecture, including Diego Rivera's Anahuacalli (1944), built in neo-Aztec style using native Mexican *tezontle* stone, or Juan O'Gorman's own house (1956, destroyed), constructed in Mexico City's Pedregal with lava blocks and decorated inside and out, floor and ceiling, with mosaics of Precolumbian themes. More recently, we may think of Pedro Ramírez Vásquez's Museum Nacional de Antropología (1964), and Félix Candela's Palacio de los Deportes (1966), with its copper-covered soccer stadium.

Since the 1960s, an important group of Mexican architects has continued to produce unique designs for both homes and public buildings. We consider Agustín Hernández and José Luis Esquerra, designers whose unique personal styles blend modernist and historical architecture.

# AGUSTÍN HERNÁNDEZ

Hernández studied architecture at Mexico's National University, graduating in 1954. During the late 1950s and 1960s, he developed a personal architectural vision based on geometry and a mixture of both futurist aesthetics and references to Mexico's Precolumbian past. His design for Mexico's main military academy, the Heróico Colegio Militar (1976), exemplifies Hernández's search for modern applications of Precolumbian art and architecture. Designed with Manuel González Rul, the vast campus of the Heróico Colegio recalls the courtyards and structural massing of Precolumbian Mexican cities like Teotihuacán, Chíchen Itzá, and Monte Alban. One structure on the campus has a façade built to look like the face of Tlaloc, the Precolumbian Aztec rain god. But unlike Aztec pyramids, which were built with rubble cores faced with veneer masonry, Hernández employs industrial materials, like steel-reinforced cast concrete and glass-curtain walls.

Hernández's designs for private homes are exercises in the sculptural possibilities of modern materials, and they seem to be plucked from the pages of science fiction novels. Hernández homes explore the plastic and volumetric possibilities of geometry, usually with only a casual nod to contemporary architectural styles. He organized the Casa Silva (1969) on a hexagonal plan, and used oval units for the Casa Betech (1981)—built with reinforced cast concrete. Hernández has even explored how traditional Mexican materials might be employed to construct buildings in his personal architectural idiom.

But Hernández's most striking homes were built on the steep hillsides of Mexico City's Lomas neighborhoods. The Hernández architectural studio (1976), and the stupendous Casa Hernández, also known as the Casa en el Aire (1988–91), cantilever some sixty feet out over the hillside, and seem impossibly suspended in the air. Industrial materials made all of these structures possible. But Hernández uses modern materials for effects completely unseen in any of the main school of contemporary Mexican architecture. His designs convey faith in the ability of futurist aesthetics to create suitable private dwellings even in challenging locations. Like his fellow Mexicans, Hernández is especially preoccupied with the locations and siting of his buildings. But his finished designs show little integration with the landscape, as we saw in the work of Luis Barragán. Instead they proclaim the ability of contemporary architecture and materials to tame and mold nature to modern living.

Page 74: Casa Betech, Mexico City, 1981. In this view
looking up from the center of the house, the dome appears
to float on a glass ribbon, evoking the great domes of
Hagia Sofia and other churches of the Byzantine world far
away from Mexico. Polished steel railings divide the interi-
or spaces of the atrium and the surrounding rooms, continuing the use of industrial materials.

Left: Casa Betech, Mexico City, 1981. A circular domed space almost thirty feet wide forms the core of the home. Four monumental columns, three inside and one outside, support the vast interior atrium.

Above: Casa Hernández, Mexico City, 1988–91. Entering this house almost requires an act of faith, since there are no windows and parking is actually beyond the edge of a cliff.

Left: Casa Hernández. A dramatic house in a dramatic setting, the architect's own home projects out into the air above a hillside in Mexico City.

Opposite: Casa Hernández. In addition to the main unit of the home, Hernández also designed living spaces on terraces below, including a swimming pool.

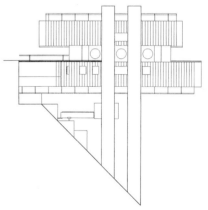

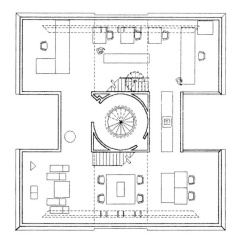

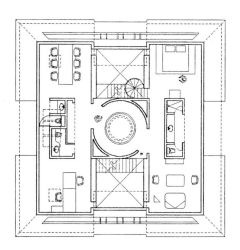

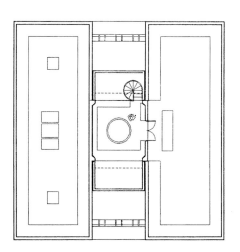

Opposite: Hernández Architectural Studio, Mexico City, 1976. Crossing a concrete bridge without railings, we enter the architect's studio, which is built on a lot inclined at 45 degrees.

Above: Hernández Architectural Studio. Hernández drew his inspiration from the support system he observed in trees. He used reinforced concrete to translate this organic form into a fantastic studio that appears to hang in space.

# JOSÉ LUIS ESQUERRA

As an architecture student at the National University of Mexico in the 1960s, José Luis Esquerra felt constrained by the unyielding features of functionalist design, then the most popular and accepted style. Esquerra instead looked to historical styles for inspiration, and he eventually developed what he called the "Lejanista style" (literally translated as "the far-away"). Esquerra's "lejanismo" evoked historical architectural styles far away in time, in place, and in the imagination. His designs for private homes, housing developments, and resorts combine aspects of Mediterranean and Moorish architecture with a healthy dose of the fantastic, which together yield a confectionary effect. Esquerra and his firm have developed a unique language of form, difficult to group with the major style trends in contemporary Mexican architecture.

Although every architect has a personal philosophy of design, Esquerra stands out for his well-developed architectural theory, complete with its own Ten Commandments: Skylines, Ensembles, Towers, Stairways, Roofs, Walkways, Water, Gardens, Patios, and Doors. He shares many of these design elements with the other architects whose homes are featured here, but his vision combines them to produce designs that cannot be confused with other Mexican architects active today. Esquerra's Lejanista style descends from Luis Barragán's concept of emotional architecture, with its emphasis on organic forms. But Esquerra looks also to the designs of Antonio Gaudí and to surrealist painters like Salvador Dalí, Leonora Carrington, and Remedios Varo. The surrealists thought that art could express the subconscious mind, the world of dreams, fantasies, and the irrational. Esquerra's designs unlock that door to the subconscious, with their towers, curving parapets, and uniquely shaped windows and skylights. Together these features defeat the hard edges of modernism. At the same time, Esquerra's Lejanista architecture draws on nostalgia for past built spaces, including those of Moorish Spain and North Africa, the Mediterranean, and the religious establishments of sixteenth-century Mexico.

Esquerra is probably best known for his Las Hadas resort in Manzanillo, Colima (1964–74), a development conceived of as a dream city, with streets, pathways, and nine prominent towers, named Water, Sun, Moon, Air, Light, Santiago, Mina, Estaño, and Trajana. Esquerra's designs for homes in Mexico, Texas, Hawaii, Spain, and Saudi Arabia share many features with Las Hadas, but all in a more intimate scale. The Villa Coral (1979) in

Santiago, Colima, has brilliant white walls, as do all Esquerra designs, and these contrast with Mexico's clear blue sky. Villa Coral lives up to its name, with uniquely shaped onion domes containing portholes and skylights that recall exotic settings. Indeed, these small domed spaces group around a swimming pool, and the whole is not far from the ocean.

Esquerra's Villas Albanas is a development of twenty-five homes built on a golf course on Horseshoe Bay in central Texas. Completed in 1980, Villas Albanas rises from the greenways of the golf course like some Moroccan palace. Albanas was Esquerra's first major project in the United States, and he found he had to import Mexican craftsmen to complete the brick vaults and domes that cover many spaces in each unit.

Villa Salamandra (1987) occupies almost two hundred feet of beachfront property in Nuevo Vallarta, Nayarit. Esquerra raised the home on a high podium to create a view and to counteract a natural depression in the sand dunes. The result is a brilliant white structure that resembles a Precolumbian temple, perched on a platform. The home features several of Esquerra's signature masonry cupolas built over living spaces on several levels. These alternate with undulating parapets and whole sections of the house that resemble sand dunes. Two swimming pools cool the terraces facing the sea, the smaller with modeled concrete crocodiles around its edge.

Esquerra's Virgo Fidelis Chapel (1995) in Chipilo, Puebla, follows the tradition of artist-designed chapels in twentieth-century architecture that includes such illustrious structures as Le Corbusier's chapel of Notre Dame du Haut at Ronchamp, France (1950–54), and Henri Matisse's Chapel of the Rosary of the Dominican Nuns (1951) at Vence, France. Mexican architects have also contributed to this tradition with such gems as Barragán's Tlalpan Chapel (1953–60) in Mexico City, and Ricardo Legorreta's Cathedral (1993) in Managua, Nicaragua. Esquerra built the Virgo Fidelis chapel for the sisters of the same order, and it perches on a ridge with a spectacular view of snow-capped volcanoes in the distance. Like other Esquerra projects, the chapel features undulating parapets and brilliant white stucco throughout. The chapel's plan continues the fantastic curves of the façade, and its footprint recalls the baroque confections of Borromini at the Roman San Carlo alle Quattro Fontane. Convents are places of retreat and solitude, and Esquerra's design lends itself to inward-turning flights of the imagination.

Page 82: Virgo Fidelis Chapel. Chipilo, Puebla, 1995. The simplicity of the chapel interior creates an atmosphere of tranquility, with regular arches resting on columns whose capitals recall those of early Christian churches. Colored light from the stained-glass windows dances across the interior walls.

Above: Virgo Fidelis Chapel. Free-form stained-glass windows light the sanctuary. From the outside, these windows interrupt the undulating façade.

Right: Esquerra punctured the chapel façade with arched openings and a bell-less belfry, features that frame the brilliant blue sky.

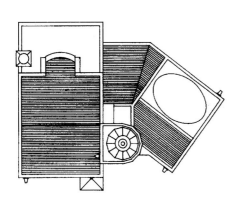
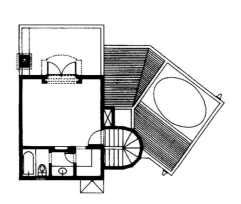
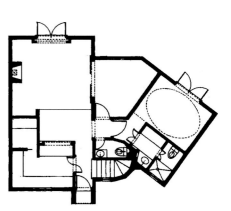

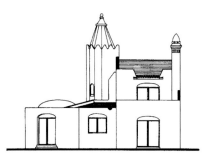

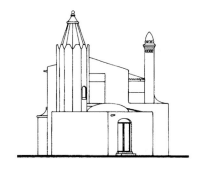

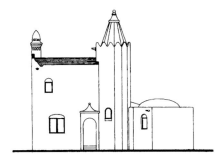

Villas Albanas, Horsehoe Bay, Central Texas, 1980. A tower dominates the front façade of the Villas Albanas.

Opposite: The end unit of Villas Albanas has a tower containing a stairway, and living spaces with patios grouped around them.

Villa Salamandra, Nuevo Vallarta, Nayarit, 1987. The play of light and shadow on the exposed underside of an interior stairway creates a shaded ledge for plants.

Opposite: Villa Salamandra. Fantasy elements in Esquerra's designs create what he calls Lejanista style, an architecture of faraway times and places.

Villa Salamandra.
The view approaching the
entrance to the Villa
Salamandra includes one
of Esquerra's signature
white towers.

Villa Salamandra.
Both walls and roof lines
undulate and break,
echoing the rhythms
of the sea.

Villa Jeddah, Jeddah, Saudi Arabia, 1994.
In this palace for a Saudi sheik, Middle Eastern fantasy
elements in Esquerra's architecture become reality.

Villa Coral, Santiago, Colima, 1979.
Onion domes with black bulging skylights cover
the rooms around one of the pools.

Opposite: Villa Coral, Santiago. Overlooking the Pacific Ocean, this palace-like house incorporates Middle Eastern elements on many levels of the living space.

Villa Coral, Santiago, Colima, 1979. Many of the patios at the villa frame dramatic views.

# FUNCTIONALISTS

The group called functionalists or Internationalists, or the modernist movement, came partly out of the Instituto de Arquitectura Mexicana, which was formed in the 1930s and has strong ties to the Bauhaus. Practical in nature, this style can be found all over the world. The giants of this movement were Walter Gropius, Eero Saarinen, Mies van der Rohe, and Le Corbusier. One of the goals of the International style, especially as it has been used in Mexico, is to reduce the costs of maintenance. In Mexico the bright sun will frequently strike all four walls of a building over the course of the year. This makes the problems of paint, glare, and heat so significant that sometimes parts of the International style simply do not work; for example, the glass-curtain wall, a hallmark of International style, has to be modified for use in Mexico, or the occupants of Philip Johnson's famous Glass House (1949 in New Canaan, Connecticut) would have been cooked on a sunny afternoon.

Another factor favoring the choice of functionalism by Mexican architects seeking an independent identity was the strong presence of the United States to the north, where the International or Bauhaus-inspired style was embraced as an answer to urban spaces. Mexican architects striving for a new architectural idiom who chose to work in the functionalist style were Abraham Zabludovsky, Teodoro González de León, Enrique Norten, Isaac Broid, Félix Sánchez, Carlos Santos Maldonado, and J. B. Johnson.

# ABRAHAM ZABLUDOVSKY

Abraham Zabludovsky studied architecture at the National University of Mexico. His schooling came at a time when there was great interest in architecture in Mexico, and the search for a national style was mixed with the desire for continuing traditional Mexican building. For architecture, it was a time of contradictions, but for Zabludovsky, the break with the past and a promise of a better way of life was compelling and helped make his decision for the modern movement in architecture. In his work, there is a desire to forget the past and move into the future. Zabludovsky wanted to join a larger world of influence and avoid the dominance of the United States. His main heroes were Le Corbusier, Mies van der Rohe, and Frank Lloyd Wright.

Zabludovsky has said, "You cannot have an architecture where structure disappears and you have no sense of how a thing stands." In particular, his work is characterized by the impeccable handling of contemporary design. He took this style from domestic to larger public buildings, a move made possible by new materials. Freed from the limitations of traditional materials, he began to create large openings and frames, which would have been impossible without the structural properties of reinforced concrete and steel I beams.

As a young architect in the 1960s, Zabludovsky did a number of residential buildings and offices in Mexico City. In 1968, he began to collaborate with Teodoro González de León, and they worked together until recently. The work they produced used functional and formal solutions that have been imitated by many other Mexican architects. Both Zabludovsky and González de León have a strong sense of design that saves their work from the boring and predictable outcome that is sometimes the case in International-style buildings. Both Zabludovsky and González de León worked to some extent with prefabricated materials. They also began to use a mixture of concrete and marble chips for exterior surfaces, which reflects the light in a subtle way.

The former partners are now rivals. While they worked together, they were a great force, combining a constructivist desire for fragmentation and heroic spans with a pre-Hispanic fascination with terraces and plazas; many of their disciples use even more refined materials and span greater spaces. Their monumental vocabulary has become almost as much a Mexican signature style as Barragán and Legorreta's bright colors.

Page 98: Sierra de la Breña Home, Mexico City, 1966. Zabludovsky built this home next to the street on a steep lot with a panoramic vista on the garden side. In the house, an elliptical study and library rises on concrete supports and connects to the second floor.

Above and right: Sierra de la Breña Home. Unlike many Mexican homes, no wall shields the house from the street. But the house walls are so blank, they function almost like a privacy wall.

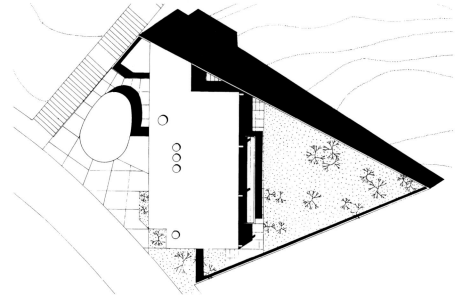

Above: Sierra de la Breña Home. Behind the house, gardens drop away into a steep sloping site. Unlike the street side, the garden façade is composed of glass walls on both stories.

Left: Zabludovsky favors industrial materials, including concrete, glass, and steel. The railings, long windows, and rooflines lend this house a strong horizontal impression.

101

Above: Zabludovsky House, Mexico City, 1969.
Like many houses in this book, Zabludovsky's home is
built on the edge of a ravine. Here he created a concrete
platform with living areas on three levels.

Above: Zabludovsky House.
The lower level from the garden shows
Zabludovsky's use of concrete and strong geometry.

103

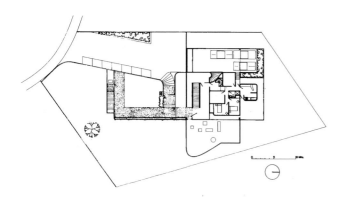

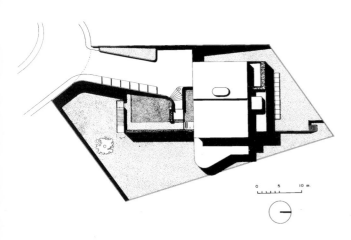

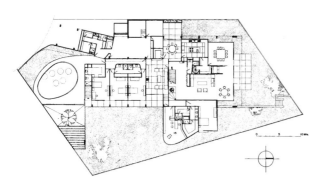

Opposite: Zabludovsky House.
A view into the living room with the
main staircase in the background.

Left: Zabludovsky House.
In American houses, stairways are
more often functional than decorative. Here Zabludovsky uses the
stairs to create a lattice pattern
and a backdrop for a Mathias
Goeritz sculpture.

105

Opposite: Apartment Remodel.
Zabludovsky's brand of international modernism
transports easily from Mexico City to New York.

Above: Apartment Remodel.
An interior view of the apartment shows
Zabludovsky's use of mirrors, which seem to
enlarge and illuminate the apartment.

Above: Private Studio, Mexico City, 1993. Built at the base
of a sloping lot, Zabludovsky used a monumental concrete
frame as the entrance to his private architectural studio.

Above: Private Studio, Mexico City, 1993. The view from the back into the studio space shows the architect's interest in using industrial materials as design elements.

# TEODORO GONZÁLEZ DE LEÓN

González de León studied first in Mexico at the Academy of San Carlos and, later, in France (1947–48) at the Le Corbusier workshop. He completed many large commissions with his former business partner Abraham Zabludovsky. His hallmark has been innovation in the use of materials and new processes. As an architect, he acknowledges his clear debt to Le Corbusier and the International style. He believes that "art is universal. It has only become local when cultures have been isolated." He often uses mathematical formulas to achieve harmony in a project.

In his work, there is an appreciation of the mild Mexican climate, and his glass walls dissolve the inside/outside boundaries so that where there is a wall, it is almost invisible. To accommodate the bright Mexican light, he pushes these walls back under portals and overhangs. Like so many Mexican architects, he uses pools, reflective or swimming, to amplify the images of his houses. His light sources are sometimes concealed, shedding light into libraries and hallways from clerestories, or hooded windows. His use of stairs for dramatic effect as well as for practical reasons is another feature he shares with other Mexican designers. In the illustrated house, Casa Amsterdam,

there are resonances of Le Corbusier's Chapel at Ronchamp. The architecture is cool and elegant with a pure line that celebrates volume. This is essentially an urban architecture.

Casa Amsterdam is in the center of Mexico City and was built in 1997. The site restricts the house but does not compromise it. It sits on an elevated platform above the street and is organized around a patio, following the common Mexican plan. Some of the buildings on the site are at slight angles to each other, more like a Maya site with astronomical alignments. The building materials are white concrete walls with marble floors. Casa Amsterdam is comprised of geometric elements, cubes, squares, cylinders, and vaults. Functional elements such as the garage are concealed under the house. This is a dwelling that might appear in any urban setting, yet has a definite Mexican character.

Opposite: González de León House, Mexico City, 1996–97. The lap pool, a common feature of Mexican homes, reflects the geometry of the house by day and by night.

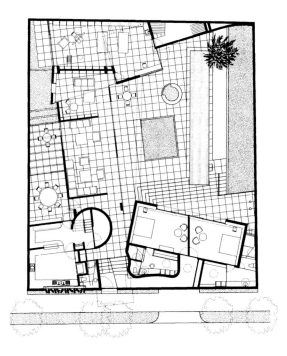

**PLANTA DE CONJUNTO**

0 1 2 3 4 5      10 MTS.

Page 112: González de León House. The architect's own home is built on a densely urbanized square-shaped lot in Mexico City. González de León designed the house as a collection of geometric elements organized around a courtyard.

Page 113: González de León House. A view from inside the artist's studio. Industrial materials allowed González de León to create the illusion that the wall hangs unsupported above the window.

Left, above and opposite: González de León House. A long concrete barrel vault covers the sitting room and library, harkening back to sixteenth-century Mexican architectural forms.

Above: González de León House. Like so many other houses in Mexico City, this home presents an opaque façade to the street. Fixed concrete louvers screen a window to the kitchen.

Above: González de León House. A view down the barrel-vaulted living room towards the library. Just beyond the glass wall on the right is a walkway roofed with glass.

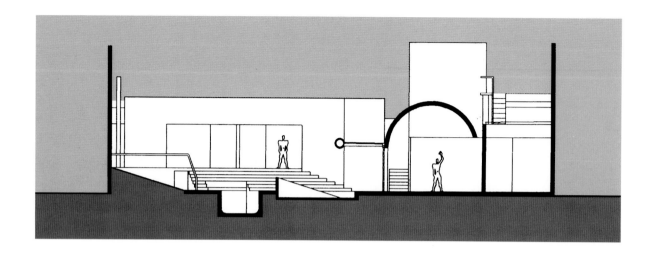

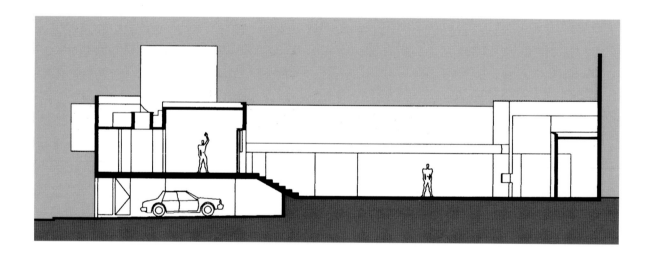

Page 118: González de León House, Mexico City, 1996–97. The library is at the end of the long barrel-vaulted space.

Page 119: González de León House, Mexico City, 1996–97. Light-colored walls and large windows provide ample light in the painting studio.

Right: González de León House, Mexico City, 1996–97. The stairwell inside the circular tower connects the parking and service areas to the main house.

Above: González de León House, Mexico City, 1996–97.
At night artificial lighting enhances the effect of the barrel
vault. The bedroom wing is visible through the glass and
across the patio to the left.

Above: González de León House. View out the living room window to the patio with a shade arbor to diffuse the bright sun.

# ENRIQUE NORTEN

Enrique Norten is one of the most prominent voices in Mexican contemporary architecture of the generation after Teodoro González de León and Abraham Zabludovsky. Norten graduated from Iberoamericana University in Mexico City in 1978, and obtained a master's degree in architecture from Cornell in 1980. With his firm—Ten Arquitectos—Norten has designed important projects in Mexico including the National Theater School (1993) and the Televisa Services Building (1995), both in the capital. He is well known for his approach to covering structures, where the roof is conceived of as independent from the walls. Norten's roofs often float on walls of glass with little obvious support. He has also been active in the United States as a design architect and as a visiting professor at the University of Pennsylvania and Cornell University. Architectural critics have compared Norten's designs favorably with those of Tadeo Ando and Richard Meier. All three share an interest in clean lines, industrial materials, and monochrome or gray interior and exterior treatment.

Norten designed the R. R. House for a sloping and partly wooded lot in the Desierto de los Leones section of Mexico City (1997). Its street façade presents a blank face of uncolored cast concrete and tan limestone panels. Windows light only the top floor on this façade and extend across the entire expanse of wall. Inside, Norten organized the house around a private courtyard with a water feature, with balconies on two floors, almost like in a colonial or nineteenth-century Mexican palace. But there the similarities end. Instead of stone or cast-iron railings, Norten's guardrails are made of brushed aluminum. They extend the length of the façade on both the second story and roof level, giving the house a horizontal effect.

Glass walls facing the interior courtyard reveal living spaces on two floors, including a study, library, and living rooms. A stairway is concealed behind an unusually shaped wing extending on one side of the garden and walled completely with frosted glass. A second-story walkway with glass floors and guardrails overlooks the double-height library and provides access to the private areas of the home behind the frosted-glass wing. With the exception of the glass walkway, Norten selected natural wood floors for use throughout the R. R. House, which help to warm the overall postmodern chill of concrete and glass. Norten also warms his homes with effective lighting, and these help to mitigate the severity of the industrial surfaces.

Enrique Norten and Ten Arquitectos design homes at the forefront of Mexican contemporary architecture in the international functionalist style.

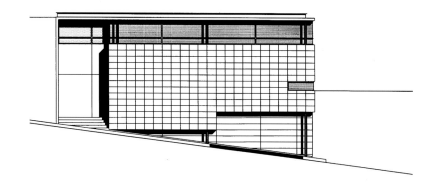

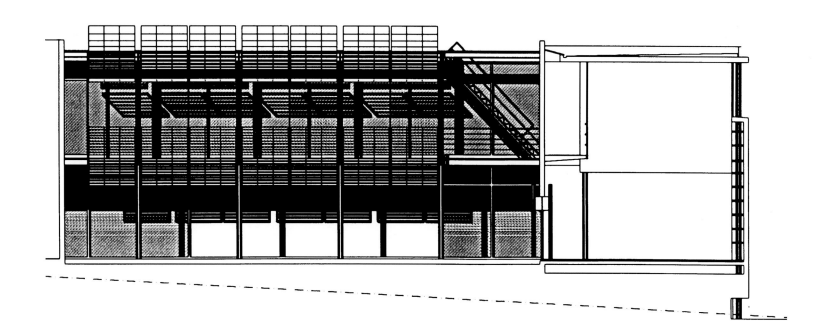

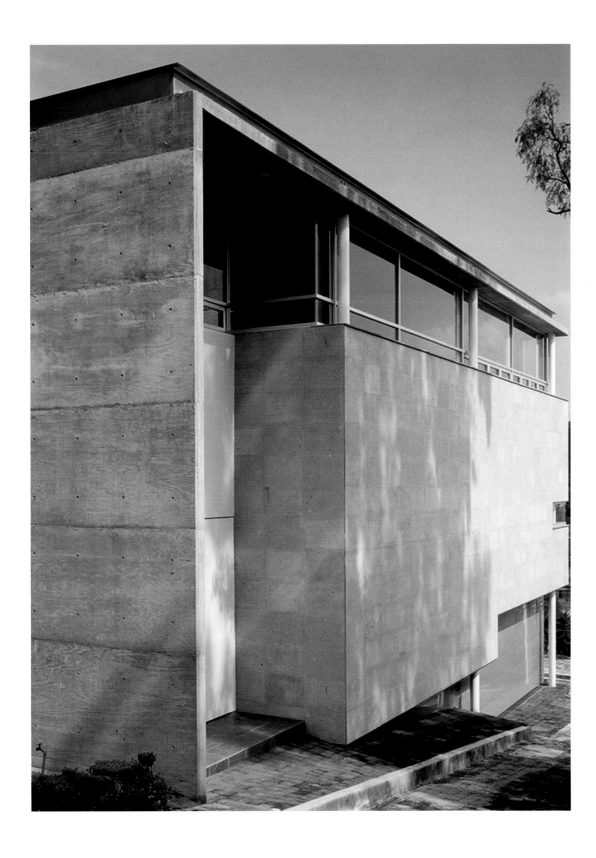

Page 124: R. R. House, Desierto de los Leones, Mexico City, 1997. View from the upper-story balcony down to the patio and across to the glass-encased stairwell.

Left: R. R. House. Built on a sloping corner lot in a dense urban setting, the massing of the house acts as a shield from the busy street.

Above:  R. R. House. The living spaces on the first and
second floors open onto a paved landscaped courtyard.

Above: R. R. House. Despite the industrial materials and stark geometry, Norten's use of lighting makes the house seem to glow from within.

Right: R. R. House.
The clean lines
of the double-
height living room
lend a sense of
transparency to the
R. R. House.

Left: R. R. House.
Designed on a small
urban plot measuring
55 x 68 feet, the
L-shaped design
maximizes the lot's
tight dimensions.

Page 132: R. R. House. A loft-like second-story room overlooks the studio and creates a guest suite.

Page 133: R. R. House. The view in the opposite direction across the glass walkway, which leads to two upstairs bedrooms and the master suite, shows the living room below.

Opposite, left: R. R. House. The spaces of this house were created by layering planes along both axes. The continuous lines of the railings and exposed floors lend the house a strong sense of horizontality.

Opposite, right: R. R. House. On the glass bridge looking into the upstairs sitting room. The patio is behind the wall to the right, and the double-height living room to the left.

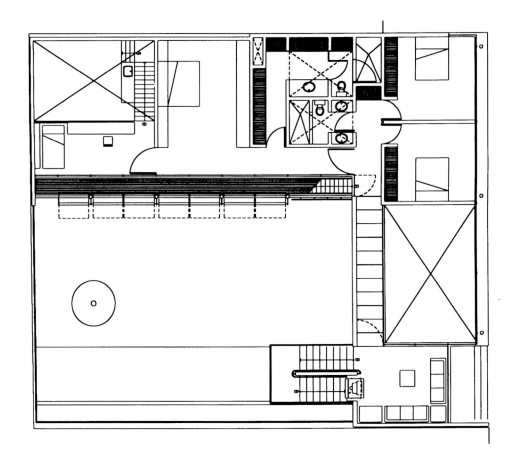

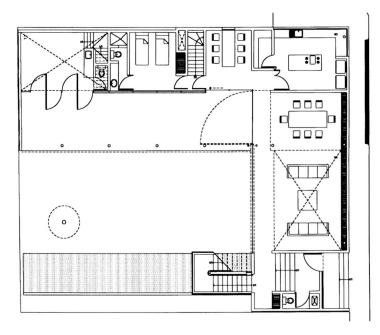

# ISAAC BROID

Isaac Broid is one of the architects who works in the functionalist style. He graduated from the Department of Architecture and Urban Planning at Iberoamericana University in Mexico City and has a master's degree from Oxford University. His works include such important public projects in Mexico City as the Centro la Imagen (1994) and a Metro Station (1990) on Line A, designed with Aurelio Nuño, et al. Among the houses he has designed are Casa Amsterdam and Casa Vasquez, both in Mexico City; Casa Fuentes, in the State of Mexico; and Casa Sodi Ambrosi, a vacation house in Puerto Escondido, Oaxaca.

Casa Amsterdam (1999) has a north-facing street façade. It follows the International canon, presenting an almost blank face to the street and giving a fortress-like aspect with a high overhanging roof characteristic of Broid. The walls are natural stone, with large windows and simple poles used for support. The glass curtain walls face gardens at the back of the house. The garage is tucked under the house and the house comes out to the street, a feature common in tight Mexican urban lots. There is a hanging staircase that is attached to the wall, one of the staircases that can never be built in the United States because of building codes; the stairs climb the wall, punctuating the stone surface in an attractive manner.

Casa Vásquez (1997) is located in Coyoacan, Mexico City, one of the prettiest districts of the capital. The functionalist style achieves harmony and balance here with quiet dignity. The house works around a garden on an almost square lot. The windows create a horizontal grid that is echoed by the second-story balcony. Light enters the center room of the house from both sides of a double-height room, which makes it very open and at the same time mysterious.

Another handsome house by Isaac Broid is Casa Fuentes (2001), a large structure with flat overhanging roofs. The top and bottom stories are glass and open, and the second or central section of the house is sheathed in stone bricks. The house has a visible exoskeleton of poles and cross bracing. The inside of the house has elements that are almost Zen; especially attractive is the low window with light seeping in almost below eye level. The feeling of this house is tranquil, and though it is clearly functionalist, it fits into the school of Barragán, who felt that a house should be a retreat.

Casa Sodi Ambrosi (1998) is a weekend house on the Pacific coast not far from Puerto Escondido, Oaxaca. Here, the climate and the site are both welcoming and nonrestricting. The house stretches along the beach and has three large bays and a somewhat taller part of the house has a generous balcony. There is a deep portal with hammocks facing the swimming pool and a garden. Here also are the stairs that go up one wall leading to the bedrooms. This house has a wonderful sense of openness and ease.

All these houses constitute a well-thought-out oeuvre that is personal and well-suited to Mexico, yet remains within the functionalist aesthetic.

Right: Casa Sodi-Ambrosi.

Page 136: Casa Sodi-Ambrosi, Zicatela, Oaxaca, 1998. Yellow hammocks punctuate the terrace. Canvas awnings offer shade and allow the sea breezes to cool the terrace and bedrooms nearby.

Opposite: Casa Sodi-Ambrosi. Another view of the distinctive canopy shading the terrace and bedrooms. The hot tropical sun beats on the canopy rather than the bedroom roof, making air conditioning unnecessary.

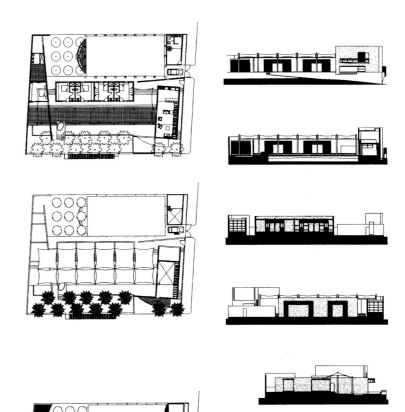

Above: Casa Sodi-Ambrosi. The openness of the outdoors is carried inside to the living room by a glass wall, light colors, high ceiling, and casual furniture.

Opposite: Casa Sodi-Ambrosi. This elegant vacation home is open to the air, and offers a pool and lap pool just outside the bedroom doors.

Top: Street façade of the Amsterdam duplex. Enclosed balconies on the upper stories offer views of the street while protecting the privacy of the inhabitants.

Bottom: Casa Amsterdam, Mexico City, 1999. The enclosed garden of the left housing unit, bordered by a glass wall that reveals a double-height living room behind.

Casa Amsterdam. The left unit's living room, with double height and a stairway to the bedroom upstairs. Broid's stairs without railings recall the designs of Luis Barragán.

Casa Amsterdam. View through the stairs into the
living room and garden. Broid combines industrial
materials with natural wood finishes.

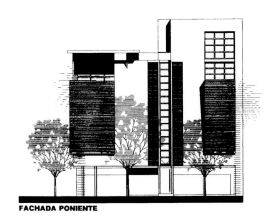

**FACHADA PONIENTE**

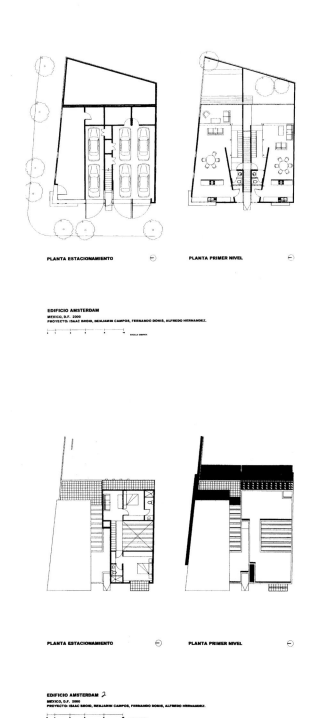

PLANTA ESTACIONAMIENTO          PLANTA PRIMER NIVEL

**EDIFICIO AMSTERDAM**
MEXICO, D.F. 2000
PROYECTO: ISAAC BROID, BENJAMIN CAMPOS, FERNANDO DONIS, ALFREDO HERNANDEZ.

ESCALA GRAFICA

**FACHADA NORTE**

**EDIFICIO AMSTERDAM** 3
MEXICO, D.F. 2000
PROYECTO: ISAAC BROID, BENJAMIN CAMPOS, FERNANDO DONIS, ALFREDO HERNANDEZ.

ESCALA GRAFICA

Casa Amsterdam, Mexico City, 1999.

PLANTA ESTACIONAMIENTO          PLANTA PRIMER NIVEL

**EDIFICIO AMSTERDAM** 2
MEXICO, D.F. 2000
PROYECTO: ISAAC BROID, BENJAMIN CAMPOS, FERNANDO DONIS, ALFREDO HERNANDEZ.

ESCALA GRAFICA

Casa Vásquez, Coyoacan, Mexico City, 1997. A view into the living room from the upstairs balcony.

Below: Casa Vásquez. Among the highlights of this house are two double-height glass walls, with an unusual fireplace nested into one of these walls in the living room.

Opposite: Casa Vásquez. View of the walled garden with the home's glass wall and second-story balcony.

Opposite: Casa Fuentes, Sayavedra, Estado de Mexico, 2001. A sundeck on the side takes advantage of the steep lot and provides dramatic views of the countryside.

Left: Casa Fuentes. The clean modernist lines of this house are mitigated by the use of rough stone and other natural materials.

Below: Casa Fuentes. A dramatic night view emphasizes the cantilevered roof overhanging a balcony, the large window in the central section of the house, and the terrace and game room at ground level.

149

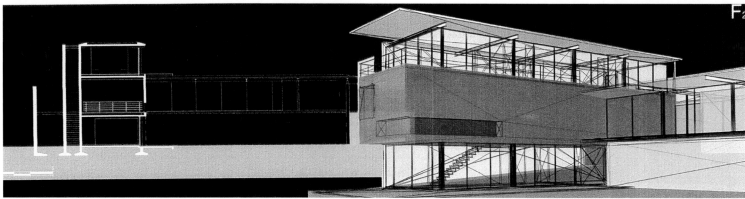

Casa Fuentes. Broid inserted a central concrete section
between the upper and lower glass levels. This floor and
the rooflines lend the house a horizontal impression.

Casa Fuentes. Inside the home's middle
level, an almost floor-level corner window
provides both light and privacy.

Chihuahua,
Mexico City, 1999.
Living spaces are
found in the front of
this unit, and are lit
by a wall of glass
with doors on
cardinal hinges.
The stairwell on the
right leads to the
upper floors.

152

# SÁNCHEZ ARQUITECTOS Y ASOCIADOS

Félix Sánchez and his associates—including Luis Sánchez, Gustavo López, Fernando Mota, and Raúl González—design a variety of projects from large public buildings to private homes that include the Historical Archives and Secretariat of Government, both in the State of Tlaxcala; a tourism center in Havana, Cuba; numerous private dwellings in Mexico, Israel, and Panama; and the Pino Suárez Market (1992), the San Ciprián Market (1989), and the graduate school of the Instituto Tecnológico de México (1991), all in Mexico City. In addition to these projects, the firm also specializes in designing duplexes and condominiums in Mexico City's tony neighborhoods, including the Colonia Roma and Colonia Hipódromo Condesa.

Sánchez and his team describe their designs as light, transparent, and luminous, and their work falls squarely in the functionalist mode. Their structures could be equally at home in Mexico City or London, deriving from an approach exactly opposite that of Barragán or his stylistic descendants. Sánchez favors walls of glass and industrial materials that present exterior façades as transparent and translucent skins. Their homes are modernist refuges, free from the mysterious spaces and blank façades of traditional Mexican architecture.

Sánchez designed the three condominium complexes presented here—Citlaltepetl, Ensenada, and Chihuahua—to fit in an urban setting between existing homes and offices. Citlaltepetl includes four units on a single lot, with shared gardens and large banks of windows on all façades. Ensenada has six row-house-style units on a corner lot. Like Citlaltepetl, these homes have living spaces on three levels, with a two-story living room lit by a large glass wall on the street façade. In addition to a garden behind it, the Chihuahua duplex includes a double carport. One of the ways Mexican homes in general differ from their American counterparts is in their treatment of garages. In Mexico, particularly in urban settings where it is not especially wise to leave cars on the street, garages are often incorporated into home designs. They are usually not the first thing one sees from the street, as in the United States, but are instead hidden behind the house or on a lower level with staff quarters. Mexican homes are self-contained units, and this approach places the designs of Sánchez and his firm within the *tradición*.

Sánchez designs his homes inside with large spaces, double heights, balconies, metal and wire guardrails, and other features that make even small homes seem airy. He prefers industrial materials, light colors, and an overall lack of moldings or any other device that could interfere with the clean lines of the design. Sánchez lights his spaces with large banks of windows, skylights, and recessed electrical fixtures that yield an industrial and modern impression. North or south of the border, his clients can rest assured of living in one of the most modern spaces available.

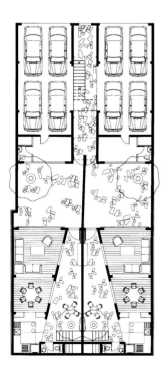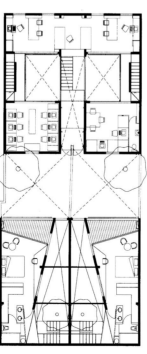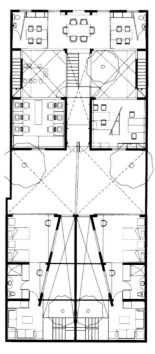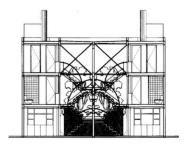

Opposite: Chihuahua. Sánchez designed the architect's studio in the rear of the unit with an open plan lit by large skylights.

Left: Chihuahua. View back through the stairwell toward the interior courtyard and office wing of the house.

Opposite, left: Chihuahua.
A stairway leads from the parking garage to the office upstairs.
The interior courtyard and
access to the house section
opens at the end of the hall.

Opposite, right: Chihuahua. A
view of the street façade shows
both units of this duplex.
Sánchez designed the window
frames with classically-inspired
postmodern features.

Right: Citlaltepetl, Mexico City,
2000. The front apartments are
organized around a central light
well that is three stories high.

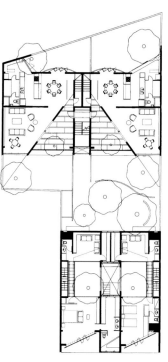

**PLANTA 2o. NIVEL**

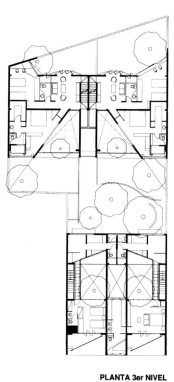

**PLANTA 3er NIVEL**

Opposite: Citlaltepetl. A view of the street façade of the two front units shows large angled bay windows with garages below.

Right: Citlaltepetl. A view down into the sitting room of one of the rear apartments. Sánchez created a garden setting in the midst of the dense urban fabric of Mexico City.

Opposite: Citlaltepetl. Rear apartment. The ground-floor sitting room is open to the interior patio.

Left: Citlaltepetl. View from one of the upstairs rooms of the rear unit into the interior patio. A glass wall lights the home and shows the garden shared with the front apartments.

Below: Citlaltepetl. Rear apartment. Unlike American homes, where dining rooms are almost always found next to living rooms on the first floor, here Sánchez lifted the dining room and kitchen to the third floor. A glass wall provides a view down to the garden.

Opposite: Ensenada, Mexico City, 2001. The second-floor view of the corner apartment shows the balcony and large skylight.

Above: Ensenada, Mexico City, 2001. Door from the patio looking into one of the other apartments. Note that the glass door turns on a central pivot, or cardinal hinge.

**PLANTA 1er NIVEL**

163

Right: Ensenada.
View of the rear
living room and
loft in one of the
middle units.

Left: Ensenada. The second-story view of one of the middle units toward the patio garden at the rear. The staircase with no railing is reminiscent of Barragán.

Above: Ensenada. A view down the hallway of the corner apartment to the window on the street façade.

Above: Ensenada. Street façade of the corner apartment, the largest of the six. Porthole-like windows and streamlined window details and a balcony are reminiscent of the French art moderne style.

# CARLOS SANTOS MALDONADO

Carlos Santos Maldonado works in the functionalist style. With architect Marisa Aja Pascual, he completed an inventive adaptive reuse of the library at the Convent of Santo Domingo in Mexico City. A good example of his domestic work is Casa de Camelia, a suburban house to the south of Mexico City near Coyoacan, where a large lot is used to maximum advantage. This house was built in the 1950s and was modernized by Santos Maldonado so that it was still a comfortable fit in an older neighborhood with established trees. Glass walls face both the street and garden areas. This house makes no gesture to the neighbors: it faces into the garden. The simplicity and elegance of the design create a private space for the family. The industrial pipe and tubing carry the structural weight and open up the house, and the addition of balconies on the second level offers access to the outside. In the project, the baths and kitchens were remodeled and an additional floor with a studio was added. The owners wanted to change the house without changing its spirit. Santos Maldonado listens to the building and to the owners with care, and does his sensitive remodels with a light touch.

Opposite: Casa de la Camelia, Mexico City (2001). Two stories of this house have glass walls facing into the garden.

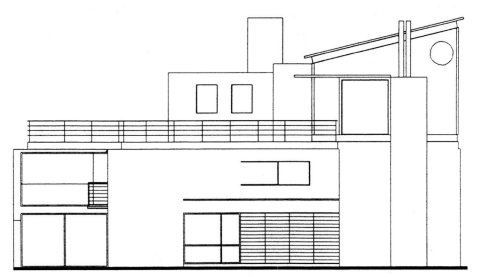

**FACHADA SUR**

Opposite: Casa de la Camelia, Mexico City. Sheer curtains on the upper level provide both privacy and light to the bedrooms. Steel railings, flat roofs, and concrete are elements of the International style that appeal to Mexican architects.

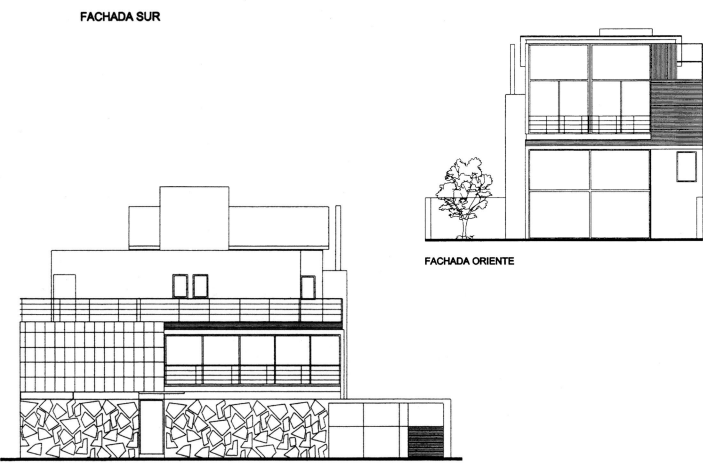

**FACHADA ORIENTE**

**FACHADA PRINCIPAL**

Left, top: Casa de la Camelia, Mexico City. A glass wall and clerestory flood the upstairs studio with light.

Left, below: Casa de la Camelia, Mexico City. The kitchen downstairs is open to the garden.

Opposite: Casa de la Camelia, Mexico City. The studio faces east, taking advantage of the morning light.

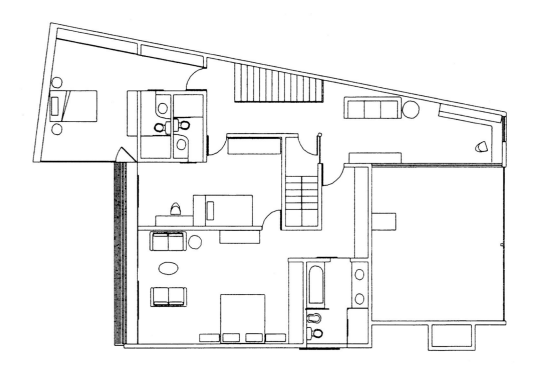

Opposite: Casa de la Camelia, Mexico City. A southern view into the studio. A small circular window and another large window frame views of the garden and the rest of the house below.

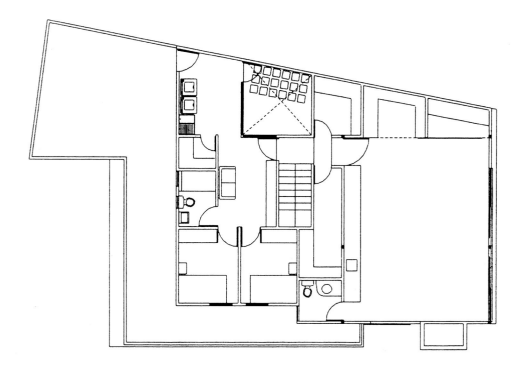

# J. B. JOHNSON

J. B. Johnson is a U.S.–trained architect who first came to Mexico in the late 1950s to restore a house in the colonial town of San Miguel Allende and has been practicing architecture in Mexico ever since. He has developed a client base consisting mostly of foreigners who fall in love with the culture, climate and typical architecture of Mexico. He works primarily in Cuernavaca, Mexico's city of eternal spring, and his homes are a direct response to his clients' desires for colonial and other exotic elements found in Mexican vernacular architecture. Johnson also responds to the benevolent climate of Cuernavaca, where there is a tendency to integrate interior and exterior spaces.

Johnson designed the Plaza del Obelisco in 1980 at the edge of a deep ravine. Originally planned for four houses, three were built with the center house straddling two lots. The interior plaza reflects the client's love for both symmetry and ancient Greek architecture. Rooms inside the house combine high ceilings with simple materials like masonry and plaster. Floors are hammered concrete and, in some cases, may be colored.

The Temixco house was built for an English gentleman devoted to Mexican art and antiques. Beginning with a small servant's house constructed with rock, a guest compound was built comprising three bedrooms with baths, a small kitchen and a large patio with space for covered dining. The main living room is a large triangular room that fits into the corner of the property with a long covered terrace overlooking a pool tiled in black mosaics. The lush plantings and large garden conceal the beginnings of major additions as part of a master plan to create a much larger home in the style of the great haciendas of Mexico's past.

Opposite: Casa en Temixco, Mexico, 1992. Johnson specializes in vacation homes for Americans in Mexico. His style reflects their interests in typical Mexican elements like patios, tile roofs, and fountains.

Page 178: Casa en Temixco, Mexico. A long reflective pool cools the patio.

Page 179: Casa en Temixco, Mexico. A narrow stairway leading to a niche with a saint sculpture contrasts with an extra-large earthenware vessel.

Opposite: Plaza del Obelisco House, Cuernavaca, Mexico, 1980-90. The smallest of the home's swimming pools is in a private patio.

Plaza del Obelisco House. Johnson designed this home on six distinct levels. A triple-height atrium occupies the center of the house.

Plaza del Obelisco House, Cuernavaca, Mexico. Large skylights light the bathroom and allow for luxuriant vegetation.

Opposite: Plaza del Obelisco House. The American-style dining and living rooms are reflected in three tall arched mirrors.

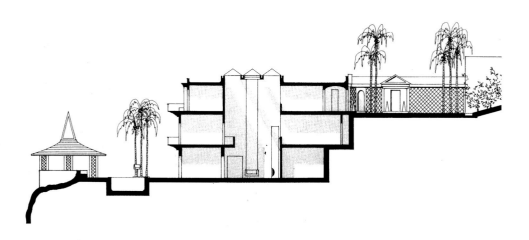

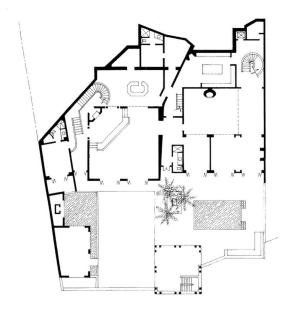

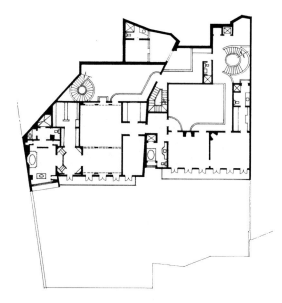

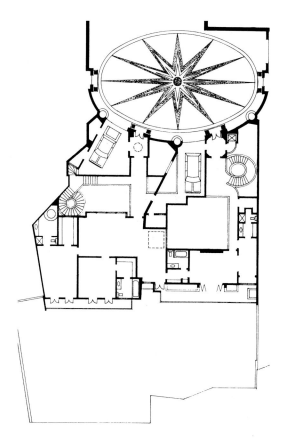

Above and left: Three levels of Plaza del Obelisco.

Opposite: Plaza del Obelisco. A fireplace is the focal point of the library.

Page 186: A large swimming pool with built-in outdoor couches overlooks a large ravine next to the house.

Page 187: Plaza del Obelisco. An oval-shaped plaza with a starburst design greets visitors to the Obelisk House. The owner admires the architecture of the ancient Mediterranean, and these interests are reflected in elements like pedimented windows and door frames.

# CONCLUSION

Although we expect a few readers will contact the featured architects to commission homes, most will use this book as a source of inspiration, as an introduction to the possibilities offered by a nearby but relatively unknown design tradition. We hope readers will realize that they do not have to build homes in the same tired styles that dominate American domestic architecture: ranch style, colonial revival, Victorian revival, and other historical styles. Housing developments in the United States are notable for their uniformity of style. We hope this book demonstrates that there are other ways of living in American cities, that the possibilities explored in this book could be used to expand conventional architectural horizons.

The introduction outlined the salient characteristics of Mexican architecture. Mexican homes, like the many presented in this book, are well adapted to their climate. They often feature covered walkways and patios that allow both inside and outside activities. Water features like pools and fountains relieve the heat of paved courtyards and provide pleasing sounds that mask urban noise. Oftentimes large glass windows and doorways can either be opened or properly oriented to shade interiors from the sun at the hottest times of the day. The last point relates to the interest in the terrain of the homesite that characterized Barragán's homes, and was continued by later Mexican designers.

Led by Frank Lloyd Wright, the United States had a brief tradition of architecture when architects carefully considered the building plot. But with the advent of modernism in the 1930s, most architects considered their designs to transcend considerations of location: the home made the site rather than the site contributing to the form of the home. Although this approach worked well with the most prominent architects, as in the case of Johnson's Glass House, it quickly degenerated in the hands of lesser talents. In the United States, homebuyers tend to purchase homes that are sited by builders to maximize the number of homes in a fixed-size development. And we wonder why our west-facing homes are so hot on summer afternoons! With the advent of modernism and the International Style, color disappeared from both domestic and commercial architecture in Europe and the United States. Le Corbusier's Villa Savoy is an early example of this phenomenon. Especially since the 1980s, architects working in the postmodern mode—Charles Moore, Michael Graves, and others—have reintroduced color in large public commissions. But this trend has scarcely touched the vast domestic architecture market. As architects like Barragán and Legorreta become better known, we are beginning to appreciate Mexican exuberance and freedom with color, especially in the American Southwest. We usually paint interior walls in light shades, a gesture sometimes intended to make rooms appear larger, and we tend to conceive of walls as backdrops for paintings and other interior décor. In contrast, Mexicans often paint their interiors in bright hues, and colored walls function as active design elements.

Mexican homes turn inward toward interior patios and living spaces, often presenting blank walls to the street. Although this phenomenon is easier to understand in dense urban settings like Mexico City, we have found it to be true even in country homes. In the introduction, we trace this inward focus back to Precolumbian architecture and also to the Mediterranean-derived courtyard homes of the colonial period. In contrast, homes in the United States place a premium upon making an impression on the street façade. Our homes have columns, ornamented doorways, and large windows that offer fleeting glimpses of interior furnishings. They often have front yards with plantings and manicured lawns that convey a sense of order and control over the natural environment. As shown in the homes presented here, Mexicans also favor gardens of various sorts, but these are almost always found inside the confines of the home. Mexican designs emphasize privacy and show little interest in impressing the neighbors or passersby.

In the United States, backyards function as family gathering spots away from the confines of the home.

Families in Mexico gather in the central patios, always hidden behind privacy walls. Mexicans also gather every day for the *comida,* the large meal of the day, served roughly at the same time Americans eat lunch. The comida and the siesta that follow are still healthy traditions south of the border, and this helps account for the importance of the dining room in Mexican homes, whereas in many American homes the dining room plays a lesser role and is often eliminated in favor of a breakfast island, larger kitchen, or combination kitchen-living room.

Many of the homes presented here were designed by the architects as collections of semiautonomous units rather than as continuous and discrete blocks. Good examples of this include the Agustín Hernández House and the González de León House. In the former, the architect built on a cliff side in Mexico City, with the main spaces of the house encased in a tubular unit cantilevered over free space. He located the pool and other support structures on the terraced hillside below, connected to the house with stairways and an elevator. And in the case of González de León, his own home is a collection of geometric forms grouped around a central patio.

And finally, we wish to mention that although most of the projects presented were designed for urban settings, a few are weekend getaways, what Mexicans call *fin de semana* homes. The homes of José Luis Esquerra and Isaac Broid's Sodi-Ambrosi House are the best examples, the latter with its emphasis on pleasure pursuits, the pool, patios, and a view of the Pacific Ocean. Weekend or second homes in Mexico often take on fantasy elements, as if both architect and client reveled in the freedom from the confines of the metropolis. One important class of Mexican weekend homes is the *palapas,* built on or near the beach with pavilions thatched with palm, or *palapas.* We did not include any of these in this book because thatch is ill-suited to building in almost every region of the United

Luis Barragán. Barragán House, Tacubaya, Mexico City. 1947–48. Barragán's use of bright Mexican colors on both interiors and exteriors established a new aesthetic in Mexican architecture that is still influential today.

States. We also felt that *palapas* homes, although very creative, failed to showcase the talents of the architects as well as their other projects.

When Americans purchase vacation or weekend homes, they often buy into an established community such as a golf course development, or in a unique area like Santa Fe, Aspen, Carmel, and Nantucket. Owning a vacation home in these communities often involves accepting existing architectural styles and community lifestyles. In contrast, Mexicans locate their weekend homes not so much in communities as in places desirable for peace.

The three authors of this book love Mexico, its traditions, and its architecture. We hope this book inspires readers to visit Mexico so they can familiarize themselves with the nation's vibrant colors, warm people, sophisticated culture, and unique architecture. Today's Mexican architects build upon foundations extending deep into the past, from Montezuma's Aztec Empire to Barragán's Mexico and beyond.

189

## PHOTO CREDITS

Introduction
Barragán House, photos by Tim Street-Porter: 20, 21, 22
Photos by J. B. Johnson: viii, 2, 3, 4, 5, 6, 7, 8, 9, 10, 11, 12, 13, 14, 15, 16, 17, 18, 19, 23, 24

Legorreta
House of 15 Patios, photos by Lourdes Legorreta: 36, 37, 38, 39
Japan House, photos by Katsuhisa Kida: 28, 30, 31, 32, 33, 34, 35

Robles
All photos by Jorge Vertiz: 40, 43, 44, 45, 46, 47, 48, 49, 51, 52, 53, 54, 55

De Yturbe
Casa in Las Lomas, photos by Amanda Holmes and Marco de Valdivia: 56, 58, 59
El Sabino Country House, photos by Christian Zavala Hagg: 66, 67, 68, 69
SY Country House, photos by Arturo Zavala Hagg: 62, 63, 64, 65

Hernandez
All photos by the Agustín Hernández Firm: 74, 76, 77, 78, 79, 80, 81, 82

Esquerra
All photos by Pedro Esquerra Borobia: 85, 86, 87, 88, 89, 90, 91, 92, 93, 94, 95

Zabludovsky
Abraham Zabludovsky Private Studio, main façade photo by Pedro Hiriart: 108
Abraham Zabludovsky Private Studio, rear façade photo by Timothy Hursley: 109
Apartment Remodel in New York, photos by Peter Paige: 106, 107
Sierra de la Breña Residence, garden view photo by Rafael: 98
Sierra de la Breña Residence, photos by Roberto Luna: 100, 101
Zabludovsky House, garden view photo by Kati Horna: 103
Zabludovsky House, photos by Julius Shulman: 102, 104, 105

De León
González de León House, photos by Luis Gordoba: 110, 112, 113, 116, 118, 119, 121, 122, 123
González de León House, photos by Pedro Hiriart: 115, 117

Norten
All photos by Luis Gordoba: 124, 127, 128, 129, 130, 131, 132, 133, 135

Broid
Casa Amsterdam, photos by Luis Gordoba: 141, 142, 143, 144
Casa Fuentes, photos by Isaac Broid: 148, 149, 150, 151
Casa Vasquez, photos by Sebastian Saldivar: 146, 147

Sanchez
All photos by Ricardo Castro: 152, 154, 155, 156, 157, 158, 159, 160, 161, 162, 163, 164, 165, 166, 167

Maldonado
All photos by Patricia Tamez: 168, 171, 172, 173, 175

Johnson
All photos by J. B. Johnson: 176, 178, 179, 180, 181, 182, 183, 185, 186, 187

Conclusion
Barragán House, photo by Tim Street-Porter: 189

# BIBLIOGRAPHY

Adrià, Miquel
1996. *Mexico 90's. Una arquitectura contemporánea / A Contemporary Architecture*, by Miquel Adrià, pp. 22–25. Ediciones G. Gil, Mexico City.

Ambasz, Emilio
1976. *Architecture of Luis Barragán.* Museum of Modern Art, New York.

Barnitz, Jacqueline
2001. "Functionalism, Integration of the Arts, and the Postwar Architectural Boom." *Twentieth-Century Art of Latin America* by Jacqueline Barnitz, pp. 166–188. University of Texas Press, Austin.

Barragán, Luis
1996. "Luis Barragán: Sitio + Superficie." *Su Obra y La Vanguardia en el Arte.* Antiguo Colegio de San Ildefonso, Mexico City.

Barragán, Luis, and Antonio Toca Fernández, Mariana Yampolsky, Alvaro Siza, and M. Buendia (contributor)
1996. *Barragán: The Complete Works.* Princeton Architectural Press, Princeton, New Jersey.

Buendía Julbez, and José María, Juan Palomar, Guillermo Eguiarte, and Sebastián Saldívar
1997. *The Life and Work of Luis Barragán.* Rizzoli, New York.

Burian, Edward R. (editor)
1997. *Modernity and the Architecture of Mexico.* University of Texas Press, Austin.

Burri, Rene
2000. *Luis Barragán.* Phaidon Press Inc., New York.

Castedo, Leopoldo
1969. *A History of Latin American Art and Architecture.* F. Praeger, New York.

Cetto, Max
1961. *Modern Architecture in Mexico.* F. Praeger, New York.

Damaz, Paul
1962. *Art in Latin American Architecture.* Reinhold Publishing, New York.

Eggener, Keith L.
2001. *Luis Barragán's Gardens of El Pedregal.* Princeton Architectural Press, Princeton, New Jersey.

Glusberg, Jorge
1983. *Seis arquitectos mexicanos.* Ediciones de Arte Gaglianone, Mexico. Includes Luis Barragán, Agustín Hernández, Ricardo Legorreta, Pedro Ramírez Vázquez, Abraham Zabludovsky and Teodoro González de León.

Haro Lebrija, Fernando de, and Omar Fuentes Elizondo (editors)
1997. *Arquitectos mexicanos: Entre la tradición y la modernidad.* Attame Editores, Mexico.

1999. *Arquitectos mexicanos: Al fin del milenio.* Editorial Arquitectos Mexicanos, Mexico.

2000. *Arquitectos mexicanos: Forma, luz y color.* Arquitectos Mexicanos Editores, Mexico.

Heyer, Paul
1978. *Mexican Architecture: The Work of Abraham Zabludovsky and Teodoro González de León.* Walker & Co., New York.

Hitchcock, Henry Russell
1955. *Latin American Architecture Since 1945.* Museum of Modern Art, New York.

Ingersoll, Richard
1996. "A Silent Reproach: Observations on Recent Mexican Architecture." *Mexico 90's. Una arquitectura contemporánea / A Contemporary Architecture* by Miquel Adrià, pp. 6–16. Ediciones G. Gil, Mexico City.

Luna Arroyo, Antonio
1973. *Juan O'Gorman: Autobiografía, comentarios, juicios críticos, documentación exhaustiva.* Cuadernos Populares de la Pintura Mexicana Moderna, Mexico.

Millon, Rene
1993. "The Place Where Time Began: An Archaeologist's Interpretation of What Happened in Teotihuacan History." *Teotihuacan: Art from the City of the Gods,* edited by Kathleen Berrin and Esther Pasztory, pp. 17–43. Thames and Hudson, New York, and The Fine Arts Museums of San Francisco.

Mutlow, John V.
1997. *Ricardo Legorreta, Architects.* Rizzoli, New York.

Pérez M., Guillermo (editor)
2000. *Arquitectura mexicana.* McGraw Hill/Interamericana Editores, Mexico City.

Plazola Anguiano, Guillermo, and Carlos Real González
1999. *50 Años. Arquitectura mexicana, 1948–1998.* Plazola Editores, Mexico City.

Ricalde, Humberto
1996. "The Recent 90's." *Mexico 90's. Una arquitectura contemporánea / A Contemporary Architecture* by Miquel Adrià, pp. 17–21. Ediciones G. Gil, Mexico City.

Riggen Martínez, Antonio
1997. *Luis Barragán: Mexico's Modern Master, 1902–1988.* Monacelli Press, New York.

Street-Porter, Tim
1989. *Casa mexicana: La arquitectura, el diseño y el estilo de México.* Noriega Editores, Mexico City. Also published in English as *Casa Mexicana: The Architecture, Design, and Style of Mexico.*

Underwood, Max
1990. "Luis Barragán: Modern Mexican Architecture." *Latin American Art* (Fall 1990): 44–49.

Yáñez, Enrique
1951. *18 Residencias de Arquitectos Mexicanos/18 Homes of Mexican Architects.* Ediciones Mexicanas, Mexico.

Ypma, Herbert
1997. *Mexican Contemporary.* Stewart, Tabori & Chang, New York.

Zanco, Federica (editor)
2001. *Luis Barragán: The Quiet Revolution.* Skira, New York.

Zúñiga, Olivia
1963. *Mathias Goeritz.* Editorial Intercontinental, Mexico.

Jorge Alessio Robles
Paseo de Las Palmas # 755
Colonia Lomas de Chapultepec
Mexico, D.F.
MEXICO c.p. 11000
(555) 520-8788
alessior@prodigy.net.mx

Isaac Broid
Ave. Mexico # 107-3
Colonia Hipodromo Condesa
Mexico, D.F.
MEXICO c.p. 11000
(555) 520-8788

José Luis Esquerra
Ahuehuetes nte. # 890
Colonia Bosques de Las Lomas
Mexico, D.F.
MEXICO c.p. 11700
(555) 251-5936 & (555) 251-6028
esquerra@data.net.mx
www.jlesquerra.com

Teodoro González de León
Amsterdam 63
Mexico, D.F.
MEXICO, c.p. 06100
(555) 286-5460
(555) 286-5578
f (555) 211-3706

Agustín Hernández
Bosques de Acacias 61
Bosques de las Lomas
Mexico, D.F.
MEXICO, c.p. 11700
(555) 596-1665
(555) 596-1065
f (555) 596-1710
agustinhdez@infosel.net.mx, aghdez@hotmail.com

J. B. Johnson
Rio Volga 17-6
Colonia Cuauhtemoc
Mexico, D.F.
MEXICO, c.p. 06500
(555) 514-7529
jaybee@prodigy.net.mx

Legorreta + Legorreta
Ricardo Legorreta
Victor Legorreta
Palacio de Versailles 285-A
Mexico, D.F.
MEXICO, c.p. 11020
(555) 251-9698
f (555) 596-6162
legorret@lmasl.com.mx

Enrique Norten
Cuernavaca #14 PB
Colonia Condesa
Mexico, D.F.
MEXICO, c.p. 06140
(555) 520-8788
schoer@tenarquitectos.com.mx
www.arquired.net/espanol/arquitectos/e_norten1.php

Sánchez Arquitectos y Asociados
Chihuahua 7
Colonia Roma
Mexico, D.F.
MEXICO, c.p. 06700
(555) 264-1056
(555) 564-1029
f (555) 574-0935
saya@df1.telmex.net.mx

Carlos Santos Maldonado
Amsterdam 266-5
Colonia Hipodromo Condesa
Mexico, D.F.
MEXICO, c.p. 06100
(555) 574-0501
(555) 574-4093
f (555) 564-0766
arqamsterdam@mexis.com

Jose de Yturbe
de Yturbe Arquitectos
Sierra Mojada 626-2
Colonia Lomas de Barrilaco
Mexico, D.F.
MEXICO, c.p. 11010
(555) 540-4368/(555) 540-4398
f (555) 520-8621
deyturbe@infosel.net.mx
www.deyturbe.com

Abraham Zabludovsky
Alcázar de Toledo # 335
Lomas Refoma
Mexico, D.F.
MEXICO, c.p. 11000
(555) 251-7720
(555) 251-7438
f (555) 251-7297
ipaz@mpsnet.com.mx

Mexico's country code from the US is 52